W9-BHU-401

Soccer

A Guide
for Players,
Coaches
and Fans

Soccer

A Guide
for Players,
Coaches
and Fans

Joe Luxbacher

Winchester Press
Tulsa, Oklahoma

Copyright ©1981 by Joe Luxbacher
All rights reserved

Library of Congress Cataloging in Publication Data

Luxbacher, Joe.
          Soccer : a guide for fans and players.

          Includes index.
          1. Soccer.   2. Soccer – Coaching.   3. Soccer – United
States.   I. Title.
GV943.L85   796.334'0973   80-26664
ISBN 0-87691-315-X

Published by Winchester Press
P.O. Box 1260
1421 South Sheridan
Tulsa, Oklahoma 74101

Book design by Quentin Fiore
Printed in the United States of America
1 2 3 4 5   85 84 83 82 81

Contents

Introduction

The world's most popular sport is finally beginning to establish itself on athletic fields throughout the United States. Soccer, internationally called "football," long considered a game to be played only in foreign lands, has taken deep root in America and at present is gaining popularity by leaps and bounds. Thousands of young players from coast to coast are choosing soccer as their sport instead of more typical American sports. High schools everywhere are adding soccer to their varsity athletic programs, and its growth has been phenomenal over the past ten years. The college scene has followed suit with more campuses elevating soccer to the varsity level.

Today, with the presence of three major professional soccer leagues in the United States, there is a great opportunity for a talented few to enter the professional side of the sport. The North American Soccer League (NASL), the American Soccer League (ASL), and the Major Indoor Soccer League (MISL) offer American players a chance to play at a high level of competition against professionals from all parts of the world. There is no longer any doubt that the future of soccer in the United States is ensured.

Soccer's present popularity may stem from the basic aspects of the sport itself. Soccer generates excitement from the opening whistle. Speed, strength, and stamina are integral parts of the game. A player need not be of any particular size or shape, but he must be a determined athlete who can react to the many situations that arise during a soccer match. A good player must quickly analyze and intelligently respond to the rapidly changing situations that occur under the pressure of match competition. It all makes for a wonderful sport to play or watch.

One question seems to puzzle most sports enthusiasts. Why, with this country's vast sports following, has soccer taken so long to arrive? This is difficult to answer. A combination of factors has delayed soccer's rise to prominence. One possible explanation might be the large number of alternative sports available. Football, baseball, basketball, tennis, swimming, and gymnastics are already established and offer formidable opposition to any sport struggling for recognition. Then, too, young people must have models. Big-name stars such as O. J. Simpson, Willie Stargell, Bobby Orr, and Bill Russell have enhanced their respective sports and influenced many young admirers. Until recently, young soccer players did not have professional superstars to idolize. Beginning with the incomparable Pelé, foreign stars such as Franz Beckenbauer, George Best, and Eusebio have graced the rosters of the American professional clubs. Native Americans such as Kyle Rote, Bob Rigby, and Ricky Davis have also gained prominence.

Soccer

As soccer continues its rapid popular growth, more young Americans are participating. This important factor ensures the future success of the sport. Even so, many of our college squads and professional club rosters are filled with skilled foreign players. This must change. If soccer in the United States is to attain major prominence on a worldwide basis, we must develop our own superstars. Skilled American-born players must comprise the major element of both our college and professional teams.

Experiencing the difficulties that face a player competing at the professional level has been enlightening to me. I found out very quickly that the aspiring professional must combine physical ability and mental attributes to survive at this level of competition. There is much more to soccer than dashing up and down the field kicking the ball.

Fortunately, through earlier exposure and improved coaching techniques, young players are gaining a better understanding and an awareness of the game that was not available in the past. The information I am passing along to young players should, if applied correctly, improve their standard of play. The youth of today are the future of the sport. They will soon realize the dream of America's rise to soccer prominence.

Joe Luxbacher

1.History

Soccer is characterized by its simplicity. It features fluid, controlled movement among players, allowing each to express his individuality within the structure of a team game. As the major sport of almost every country on every continent except North America, it provides a universal language among countries and their peoples, a common tie that transverses political, cultural, and religious barriers. Although the sport has undergone many modifications since its beginning, soccer truly remains the sport of the masses.

The actual origins of the game are difficult to determine. A forerunner of modern soccer originated in Greece and was called *episkyres*. A somewhat similar game, using a leather ball, was played in China possibly as early as 200 B.C. The basics of the sport gradually spread to the Roman Empire and took the form of a ball-carrying game called *harpustum*. An oval object, often the inflated bladder of an animal, was kicked, punched, or carried toward a designated goal. Early matches usually took place between two rival towns several miles apart, with the town marketplaces serving as goals. Rules were not strictly enforced and were considered of no particular importance. The games sometimes lasted several days, crossing rugged terrain and an occasional river. The Roman version of the sport was actually a combination of soccer and rugby, since use of the hands to propel the ball was permitted. In essence, modern soccer is a derivative of these ancient games, but its development was nurtured in medieval Britain.

Initially, the British version of the game was associated with the celebration of yearly festivals. As its popularity increased, play became more widespread and was no longer limited to holidays or festive occasions. The sport only vaguely resembled that which is played today.

According to legend, King Edward III became upset because his troops preferred to play soccer rather than engage in warfare, and in the fourteenth century the king prohibited play by the military. Ironically, the British military later played a major role in introducing the sport throughout the globe in the late 1800s, during which the expansion of the British Empire was at its height.

Soccer gradually spread through the public schools of England and the eventual result was the formation of the first soccer club, Sheffield, in 1857. Until that time, the rules of the game were somewhat flexible, depending on the fancies of the players involved; the use of the hands was often allowed. The Sheffield club prohibited the use of hands, and so the initial division between the sports of soccer-football and rugby-football was made. However, the basic rules still lacked uniformity in different areas of the country with teams using eleven, twelve, or fifteen players per side. In 1870, a law restricting the club to eleven players per side was enacted and the first attempt at organizing team members into strategic playing formation occurred.

Soccer

A significant event in the early history of the sport was the formation of the London Football Association in 1863. Representatives of eleven clubs, all favoring the kicking form of the game, met at the Freemason's Tavern in London and voted to confine play entirely to kicking and heading. To distinguish between the two forms of football, one was called rugby and the other designated as association football, later shortened to assoc and eventually to soccer. Many more associations were formed in the different countries after the meeting of the London Football Association. An international body became a necessity, and in 1904 the Fédération Internationale de Football Association (FIFA) first met and organized in Paris.

Today there are more than 140 member nations in the world body. Many of these countries participate in World Cup competition, an international tournament that decides the championship of the soccer world. Initiated in 1930 and held every four years, it is considered by many to be the world's most prestigious sporting event, attracting a huge following from all over the globe. Elimination rounds determine group finalists who meet at predesignated sites in a selected country to determine an ultimate winner.

As time passed, the game spread beyond the confines of Great Britain. During the latter part of the nineteenth century, with a greater number of countries participating, many innovative rule changes were made in an attempt to standardize play among the various associations. In 1872 the size of a regulation ball was defined, crossbars over the goalmouth were authorized in 1875, and an initial mention was made of goalkeepers being permitted the use of hands to control and distribute the ball. Still in its infancy, the game was played by amateurs; professional teams had not yet surfaced. In 1885 professional soccer was legalized in England.

Since soccer has only recently gained national exposure in the United States, many people incorrectly believe the game has been played here only in comparatively recent times. This idea is far from true. Soccer has been played here for the past century, possibly as early as 1830. In fact, the interest and enthusiasm of small-town players and fans in various sections of this country has provided the strong impetus needed to keep the sport alive. In many instances, soccer has been ethnically oriented, forming many intense and long-standing rivalries. Collegiate soccer has also been in existence for quite some time, with a number of schools putting soccer on their sports agenda toward the end of the nineteenth century. The first official collegiate match is reported to have occurred between Princeton and Rutgers in 1869. During the early years of the twentieth century, a steady stream of European immigrants helped to foster interest in the sport. In any event, amateur soccer has sustained the game through lean times since the turn of the century.

Along with the growth of the sport in the United States, a new problem developed. To bring the various leagues in this country under the uniform system of rules and regulations of

Courtesy Tulsa Roughnecks.

the international body, a national governing body had to be formed. In 1913, the United States Soccer Football Association (USSFA) was organized and approved by FIFA. Since then, the association has changed its name to the United States Soccer Federation (USSF). The tremendous increase in youth soccer participation has resulted in the establishment of USYSA, the United States Youth Soccer Association, an affiliate of the USSF.

Soccer

During its tumultuous history in the States, the game experienced peaks and valleys in its progress. One of its finest hours occurred on June 27, 1950, when the United States team stunned the world by upsetting England 1-0 in World Cup competition at Belo Horizonte, Brazil. Many believed that the win would make the sport an immediate success in the U.S., but such was not the case. Progress, although steady, was slow in coming.

An important element in the development of the game in the United States was the introduction of major professional soccer leagues to the public. Although the American Soccer League had been in existence for many years, it had never received the acclaim and recognition usually accorded a professional sport. In 1967 a major attempt to establish professional soccer began with the formation of two leagues. The United Soccer Association fielded teams in twelve cities and the National Professional Soccer League began with ten franchises.

Initially, the leagues faced many problems. A heavy reliance on imported talent proved costly and, coupled with low attendance figures, caused both leagues to suffer financial setbacks. In an attempt to consolidate their efforts, the two leagues merged into the North American Soccer League (NASL) in 1968. The new league gained in stability, and attendance slowly increased. Today, the NASL is firmly established with franchises throughout the United States and Canada. Crowds in excess of 70,000 have packed the Meadowlands Stadium to view the New York Cosmos and their host of international and American stars. Other successful teams, all sporting colorful nicknames, include the Tampa Bay Rowdies, Tulsa Roughnecks, Seattle Sounders, and Dallas Tornado, to name only a few. Since its formation in 1968, the league has expanded to more than twenty teams, which are presently divided into the National and American conferences. The league's recent success is, in part, a result of the increased use of television as a means of selling the game. Millions of Americans who had no previous direct contact with professional soccer were able to view the sport for the first time from their own living rooms.

Professional indoor soccer has burst on the nation's sports scene and could possibly rival outdoor soccer as the sport of the future. Although the rules differ somewhat from the traditional, indoor soccer provides a fast-paced, high-scoring game that appeals to the American sports fan. The Major Indoor Soccer League (MISL), established in 1978, has already undergone expansion and has demonstrated steady increases in overall attendance.

Paralleling and even surpassing the popularity growth of professional soccer in the United States has been a phenomenal increase in participation at the youth level. Thousands of boys and girls are now playing in organized leagues throughout the country. Traditionally considered a game played only by men, soccer is now reported to be America's fastest-growing women's sport with more than 100,000 female participants in organized leagues (however, for consistency, masculine pronouns have been used throughout the text). In addition, a Special Olympics program offers handicapped children the opportunity to play and enjoy the game. Soccer is truly becoming established in all segments of the population as more people discover the benefits and the enjoyment that it offers.

Courtesy Tulsa Roughnecks.

2. Laws and Equipment

FIFA Laws *

The laws governing soccer have been issued by FIFA and apply to all competitions involving teams affiliated with FIFA, with the exception of a few rule variances in the American pro league. It is necessary to have a uniform system of laws since the game is international in nature. Teams located in different areas of the world playing under a variety of self-imposed rules would seriously hinder international competitions. To derive the greatest enjoyment from the game, players and fans alike should have a complete understanding of the laws governing play.

Field of Play

The soccer field is a large, rectangular playing area. The length may vary from 100-130 yards and the width 50-100 yards. International matches limit the length to 110-120 yards and the width to 70-80 yards. In all cases, the length of the field must exceed its width.

The area of play is marked by distinctive lines, not more than 5 inches in width. The side boundaries of the field are called touchlines or sidelines, and the boundaries at the ends of the field are called goal lines.

The **goal area** is a rectangular area at each end of the field of play. Two lines are drawn at right angles to the goal line, 6 yards from each goal post, and extend onto the field of play for a distance of 6 yards. These two lines are joined by a line drawn parallel to the goal line.

The **penalty area** is also a rectangular area at each end of the field of play, with lines drawn at right angles to the goal line 18 yards from each goal post. These two lines extend 18 yards onto the playing field and are connected by a line drawn parallel to the goal line. The goalkeeper is permitted to handle the ball within the penalty area. The **penalty spot**, located within the penalty area, is marked 12 yards in front of the midpoint of the goal line. Penalty kicks are taken from this spot. The **penalty arc** is a line located front-center of the penalty area, having a radius of 10 yards from the penalty spot. All players, except the kicker and goalkeeper, must remain outside of the arc while the kick is being taken.

The **corner area** has a radius of 1 yard, marked at each corner of the field. When the defending team kicks a ball out of bounds over its own goal line, the opposition is awarded a kick taken from the nearest corner.

* The basis for the material in this chapter was taken from the FIFA laws.

Soccer

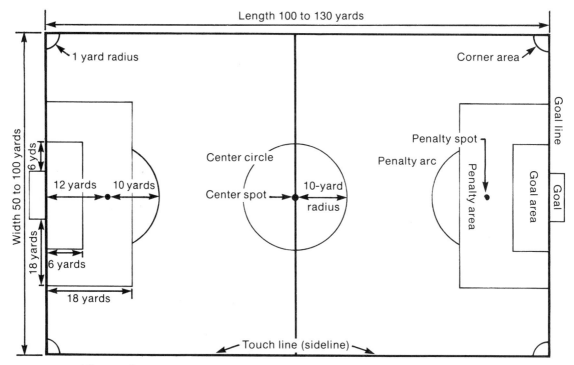

The **goals** are located on the center of each goal line. Their dimensions are 8 feet high by 8 yards wide.

The **center circle**, with a radius of 10 yards, is drawn in the center of the playing field. The midpoint of the circle is called the **center spot**, located on the halfway line. After a goal is scored and at the beginning of each half of play, the game is restarted by a kickoff from the center spot. Only the team kicking off may be in the circle prior to the kickoff.

The Ball

An official soccer ball must be spherical and made of leather or other approved materials. The circumference can vary from 27–28 inches and the weight 14–16 ounces. During play, the ball should not be changed unless authorized by the referee.

The Players

A soccer game is played by two teams, each consisting of eleven players. One of the eleven must be designated as the goalkeeper and is allowed to use his hands within the penalty area. A variety of tactical systems of play have been implemented throughout the long history of the game and are constantly changing. The actual organizational alignment of players on the field is becoming less defined, since modern soccer emphasizes mobility and the ability of players to play both defensive and attacking roles.

Referees and Linemen

A soccer game is officiated by a referee assisted by two linemen. The referee enforces the laws during play and is the ultimate authority of the field. The linemen are positioned on opposite sides of the field. They indicate when the ball is out of play and determine which side is entitled to the throw-in, goal kick, or corner kick. They also aid in signaling offside violations.

Duration of the Game

The game consists of two equal periods of 45 minutes each. A 5-minute halftime break is taken between periods. Youth games may consist of shorter periods by agreement.

Start of Play

To begin play, a toss of the coin decides choice of ends and also which team kicks off. The game is started by a player taking a placekick from the center spot into the opponents' half of the field of play. Every player must be in his own half of the field and every player of the opposing team must be at least 10 yards from the ball until the kickoff. The ball is not in play until it travels forward the distance of its circumference and cannot be played a second time until it has been touched by another player. The game is restarted in the same manner after a goal and also after halftime.

Ball In and Out of Play

The ball is considered out of play when it has wholly crossed the goal line or touchline, whether on the ground or in the air. It is out of play only when the game has been stopped by the referee. At all other times the ball is considered in play, including:

- Rebounds from a goalpost, crossbar, or corner flagpost onto the field of play.
- Rebounds off either the referee or linemen when they are in the field of play.
- Until a decision is given for an infringement of the rules.

When the referee cannot determine who last touched a ball that travels out of bounds, the game is restarted with a drop ball at the spot where the ball was last in play. The referee drops the ball between two opposing players who attempt to gain possession of the ball after it has touched the ground.

Methods of Scoring

A goal is scored when the entire ball has passed over the goal line, between the goalposts, and under the crossbar – provided it has not been carried, thrown, or intentionally pro-

Soccer

pelled by the hand or arm of an attacking player. Each goal scored counts for a single point during the course of a match, and the team scoring the most goals is the winner. If the game ends with an equal number of goals scored by both teams, it is termed a draw.

Offside

A player is offside if he is closer to his opponents' goal line than the ball is at the moment the ball is played unless:

- He is in his own half of the field of play.
- Two of his opponents are nearer to their own goal line than he is.
- The ball last touched an opponent or was last played by him.
- He receives the ball directly from a goal kick, a corner kick, a throw-in, or when dropped by the referee.

A player in an offside position is not penalized unless, in the opinion of the referee, he is interfering with the play or with an opponent or is seeking to gain an advantage by being in an offside position. Punishment for an infringement of the offside law is an indirect free kick awarded to a player of the opposing team from the place where the infringement occurred.

Offside is not judged at the moment the player in question receives the ball but at the moment the ball is passed to him by a member of his own team. A player who is not in an offside position when one of his teammates passes the ball to him does not, therefore, become offside if he goes forward during the flight of the ball.

The North American Soccer League (NASL) has a unique offside rule that differs slightly from the traditional view of offside. The NASL has adopted an offside line located 35 yards from each goal, rather than at midfield. Forwards can station themselves 35 yards from their opponents' goal without being offside, regardless of where the defending players are located. However, once inside the offside line the traditional offside rules take effect.

One of the criticisms of professional soccer in recent years has been the limited amount of scoring and the overemphasis on defense. The rule change was designed to increase the number of goals scored in a typical NASL game. It gives attacking players an advantage since they no longer have to be concerned with offside violations unless they are within 35 yards of the opponents' goal. Defending players can no longer count on an offside call from the referee when a forward positions himself behind the defense. However, since implementation of the 35-yard line, the total number of goals scored per game in the NASL has not significantly increased, probably because modern defenses have successfully adjusted to the change.

Fouls and Misconduct

When a player commits a foul or some other form of misconduct, the opposing team is awarded a free kick as a result of the illegal play. A direct free kick is assessed for intentionally:

- Kicking or attempting to kick an opponent.
- Tripping an opponent.
- Jumping at an opponent.
- Charging an opponent in a violent or dangerous manner.

Soccer

- Charging an opponent from behind unless the latter is obstructing.
- Striking or attempting to strike an opponent.
- Holding an opponent.
- Pushing an opponent.
- Handling the ball (except for the goalkeeper within his own penalty area).

If a defending player intentionally commits one of these offenses within his own penalty area, a penalty kick is awarded to the opposing team. Indirect free kicks are awarded as a result of the following infractions:

- Playing in a dangerous manner.
- Charging with the shoulder when the ball is not within playing distance of the players involved; not playing the ball.
- Intentional obstruction of an opponent when not playing the ball.
- Charging the goalkeeper except when he is holding the ball, obstructing an opponent, or has passed outside of his goal area.
- When the goalkeeper has taken more than four steps while holding or bouncing the ball without releasing it to be played by another player, or used tactics with the intention of delaying the game and as a result giving his team an unfair advantage.

Free Kicks

Free kicks are classified into two groups: direct and indirect. A goal can be scored directly against the offending side on a direct kick, while an indirect kick cannot be scored unless the ball is touched by a player other than the kicker before passing through the goal.

Opponents must remain at least 10 yards from the ball until it is played. The ball is considered in play after it has traveled the distance of its own circumference, and it must be stationary when the kick is taken. If the kicker plays the ball a second time before it has been touched by another player, an indirect free kick is awarded to an opponent from the spot where the infringement occurred.

Penalties

When an infringement of a law is detected, it is the responsibility of the referee to punish the guilty team. Since the severity of fouls varies, the degree of punishment is flexible.

Yellow- and red-card violations. If a referee decides to officially caution a player, he holds up a yellow card. The caution is a warning to the player that a repeat of the original offense, or another flagrant violation, will result in expulsion from the game.

Soccer

When the referee elects to eject a player from the field of play, he holds up a red card to signal the violation. A player may be sent off the field for any of the following offenses: (1) violent conduct or serious foul play, (2) foul or abusive language, or (3) persistent misconduct after receiving a caution (yellow card) from the referee.

Once a player has been expelled from the game, he may not return and cannot be replaced by a substitute. The card system is an effective means of limiting violent or dangerous conduct in soccer.

Penalty kicks. If the defending team commits a major infraction of the laws within its own penalty area, the opposition is awarded a penalty kick to be taken from the penalty mark. The goalkeeper must stand with both feet touching the goal line, between the goal posts. He is not permitted to move his feet until the ball has been played. A goal may be scored directly from a penalty kick. If necessary, the time of play is extended at halftime or fulltime to allow a penalty kick to be taken.

Throw-in. When the ball passes over a sideline, either on the ground or in the air, it is put back into play by a throw-in at the point where it crossed the line. The player who throws in the ball must face the field of play and part of each foot must be either on the sideline or on the ground outside the sideline. The ball must be held in both hands and delivered from behind and over the head. As soon as the ball enters the field of play, the ball is considered in play, and the thrower cannot touch the ball again until it has been played by another player. A goal cannot be scored directly from a throw-in.

Goal kick. When a ball is last touched by the attacking team and passes over the goal line, excluding the line between the goal posts, either on the ground or in the air, a goal kick is awarded to the defending team. The kick is taken from within the goal area nearest to where it crossed the line. The ball must travel beyond the penalty area before it is touched by another player; otherwise, the kick is retaken. The kicker cannot touch the ball a second time until it has been played by another player. Opposing players must remain outside of the penalty area until the kick is taken. A goal cannot be scored directly from a goal kick.

Corner kick. When the ball has been last played by the defending team and crosses the goal line, excluding the portion between the goal posts, either in the air or on the ground, a corner kick is awarded to the attacking team. The kick is taken from the nearest corner area within the quarter circle. A goal may be scored from a corner kick. Opposing players must remain at least 10 yards from the ball until it is played. It is illegal for the kicker to play the ball twice unless it has first been touched by another player.

FOUL

Intentional tripping

Pushing

Use of elbow

Dangerous play

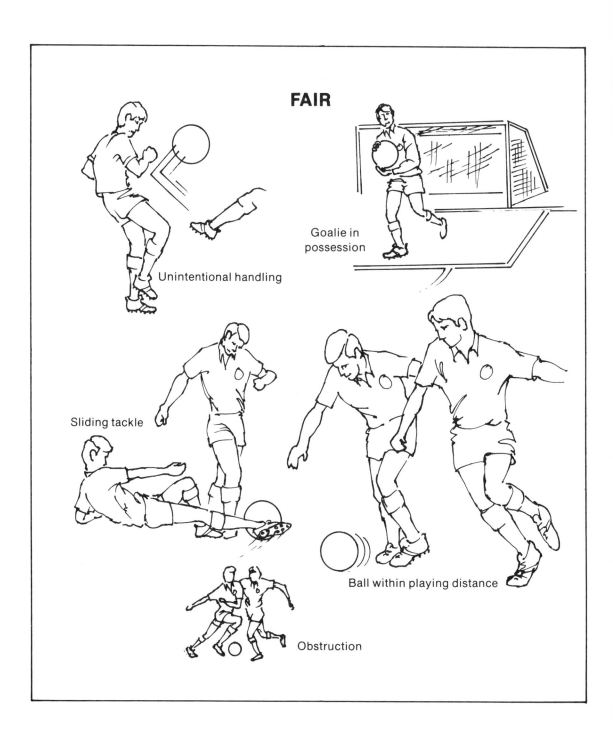

FAIR

Unintentional handling

Goalie in possession

Sliding tackle

Ball within playing distance

Obstruction

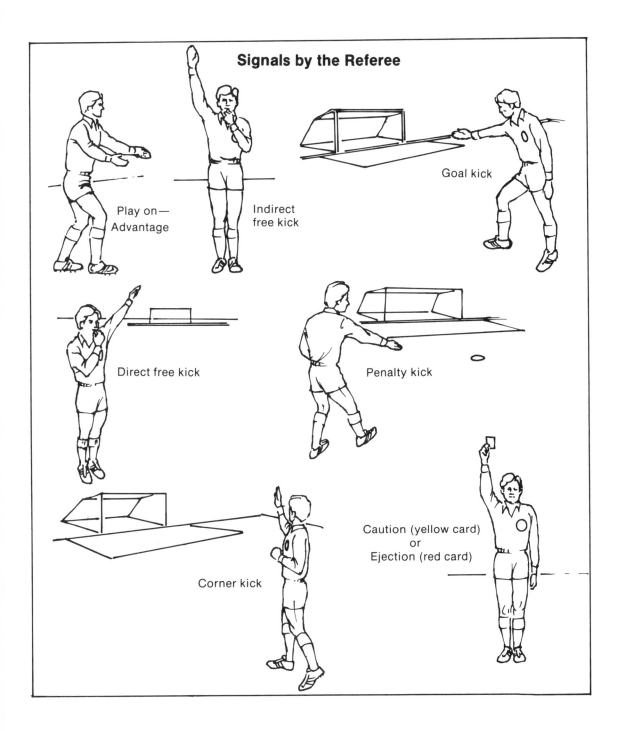

Signals by the Referee

Play on— Advantage

Indirect free kick

Goal kick

Direct free kick

Penalty kick

Corner kick

Caution (yellow card) or Ejection (red card)

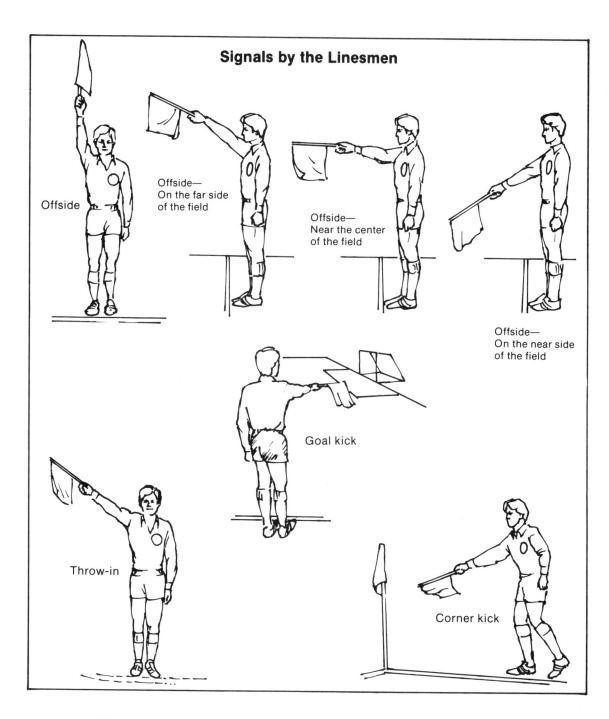

Signals by the Linesmen

Offside

Offside—
On the far side
of the field

Offside—
Near the center
of the field

Offside—
On the near side
of the field

Goal kick

Throw-in

Corner kick

Official's Signals

When the referee or linemen observe a violation of the laws, they will signal the offense with a variety of hand and body movements. These FIFA signals are designed to inform players and spectators of the referee's decision. The signals that are illustrated are those most often used by the referees and linemen.

Indoor soccer is governed by a different set of rules than outdoor soccer. The Major Indoor Soccer League has developed its own system of referee's signals, and they are shown in the chapter on indoor soccer.

Scoring Systems

The traditional international method of scoring points in league standings is the awarding of two points for a win, one point for a draw, and zero points for a loss. For example, a team with a record of 5 wins, 2 losses, and 3 draws would total 13 points. There are no bonuses given for scoring goals. The American professional leagues have adopted different scoring systems in an attempt to promote more goal scoring.

The North American Soccer League determines its league standings based on six points for each win, none for a loss, with one bonus point given for every goal scored up to a maximum of three per team per game. No bonus points are awarded for either an overtime goal or shootout goal.

The NASL has adopted a unique tie breaking method, the shootout, in the event that a game ends in a draw after the overtime period. Each team selects five players to participate in a shootout. The ball is placed on the 35-yard line and each player, on signal by the referee, has 5 seconds to dribble toward the goal and score. The team that scores the most goals out of five attempts wins the game.

The American Soccer League scoring system differs slightly from the NASL. Five points are awarded for a win, two points for a tie, and one bonus point for each goal scored up to a maximum of three per team per game.

Equipment

One reason for soccer's acceptance in the junior and senior high schools, as well as colleges, is its relatively low cost of operation. Very little equipment is needed compared with football or hockey. Shoes, ball, and a pair of gym shorts are really all one needs to play. Goalkeepers require their own specific types of equipment since they are the specialists on the team. Certain other forms of equipment, such as shin guards and athletic supporters, are useful for preventing injuries.

NASL Referee Signals

Offsides—arm moves across body indicating team offside

Indirect free kick

Directional signal

Time allowance

Pushing

Unfair tackle from behind

Striking (clenched fist)

Caution/ ejection

Handling

Play on— Advantage

Restart clock

Foul throw

Retire 10 yards

Stop the clock

Shoes

A soccer player's shoes should be his most prized possession. Just as a baseball player makes a living with his glove, the soccer player must take special care of his feet since they are the tools of his trade. A variety of shoes are available, ranging from low-priced economy models to very expensive styles. It is important that each player select shoes that are comfortable and lightweight. Multistudded soles are common today since they can be used on both natural and artificial turf. The screw-in studs are most effective on heavy, wet fields since the longer spikes provide added traction. They are not often used on hard or artificial surfaces since they limit traction and could possibly result in injuries.

Lightweight training flats, usually made of leather, are used for indoor soccer. They may also be worn for outdoor training if the playing surface is dry and provides solid footing.

Balls

Each soccer player should have access to his own ball. Many forms of technique training, such as ball juggling, passing, shooting, and dribbling, can be accomplished without a partner.

A variety of soccer balls is available on the market, ranging from lower-priced synthetics to expensive leather models. The regulation-size ball for adult players is a #5. Beginners sometimes prefer a smaller ball (size #4), which is lighter and has a circumference of 25-26 inches.

Shin Guards

Light, protective shin guards should be worn to protect the lower leg area. Most are inexpensive, and they serve a protective function in the event a wild kick lands on the shin bone. Contrary to popular belief, shin guards do not hinder a player in his movements or his ability to perform in the match.

Goalkeeper's Equipment

The goalkeeper is the one true specialist on the soccer field. Since he must perform acrobatic movements in his attempts to prevent goals, oftentimes crashing heavily to the ground, the goalkeeper's uniform must have additional padding.

The typical shirt is long sleeved with padding at the elbows and on the chest. Goalkeeper shorts are also padded in the hip areas to prevent bruises to the hip joint. Additional equipment may include elbow and knee pads as long as they do not restrict flexibility and overall movement. Male goalkeepers often wear a protective, plastic cup to prevent injuries to the groin.

Soccer

A ball, good shoes and shorts are the only necessary equipment for a soccer player.
Shirt, shin guards, and headband are optional.

Many goalkeepers choose to wear special gloves, especially when weather conditions are less favorable. Various styles are available, including leather, cotton, wool, and nylon. It is important that the gloves fit comfortably and provide a solid grip on the ball.

3.The Players

Soccer is a team game. Eleven players meshed into one functioning unit – running, passing, shooting, all striving toward an ultimate goal. Even though soccer revolves around a team concept, in actual competition the game is composed of many individual confrontations. The team that wins the majority of the one-on-one situations will usually find a successful result. Therefore, each player must master the skills that will enable him to contribute to his role within the team structure.

In the past, positional play was far more restricted than in the modern version of the game. Fullbacks were regarded strictly as defenders, forwards only as attackers. The mere thought of a defender rushing the length of the field for a shooting attempt on the opposing goal would have sent most coaches to an early retirement. Visions of a forward defending within his own penalty area were equally outrageous. All that has changed, however, with the evolution of the sport. Soccer is now a game of total involvement in which each player must be able to play all positions. Modern tactics require players to develop both attacking and defending capabilities. Even so, each position within the team has basic attributes associated with it.

Goalkeeper

The keeper may be the loneliest man in the park. He is, in reality, the last defender – the final barrier that the opposing team must conquer in order to score. He protects a goal 24 feet wide and 8 feet high. When his team has been scored against, the goalkeeper invariably receives the brunt of the criticism even though he may not actually be at fault. It is a demanding position and usually takes a special kind of athlete to accept the challenge.

A number of basic qualities are characteristic of the more successful goalkeepers. Quickness is a definite asset, both physical and mental. The ability to act, whether it be a booming drive from outside the penalty area or a close-in deflected shot, is essential for top-class netminders. Mental quickness – recognizing a situation as it arises and acting accordingly – enables the goalkeeper to position himself to the best possible advantage. The mental aspect of the sport is often neglected, but it plays a major role.

Anticipation, the uncanny ability to predict the movement of opponents, provides an added advantage for the goalkeeper. The ability to anticipate may evolve naturally for some players, but for many it is acquired only through diligent study of an opponent and the game.

Scottish-born defender John Gorman, "Gallopin' Gorman" of the Rowdies, races to gain possession of the ball. *Courtesy Tampa Bay Rowdies. Photo by Richard Steinmetz.*

A Minnesota Kick fouls a Ft. Lauderdale player while battling for possession of the ball. *Courtesy Minnesota Kicks. Photo by Fred Anderson.*

Gus Moffet of the Detroit Express eyes the ball for a downfield pass. *Courtesy Detroit Express. Photo by Steve Erznoznik.*

Mick Poole of the Portland Timbers performs a goal kick. *Courtesy Portland Timbers.*

A Houston Hurricane passes the ball to a teammate in a better scoring position. *Courtesy Houston Hurricane. Photo by William LoDato.*

Rowdie Captain Jan Van Der Veen and Cosmos Giorgio Chinaglia vie for control of the ball. *Courtesy Tampa Bay Rowdies. Photo by Richard Steinmetz.*

"Iron Mike" Connell of the Tampa Bay Rowdies defends his goal from an airborne pass. *Courtesy Tampa Bay Rowdies. Photo by Robert S. Spann.*

Another important characteristic is the basic personality of a goalkeeper. He must be courageous. Probably the roughest physical action of the entire game occurs in the goal area, and the netminder may become involved in bone-shaking collisions. He must have the courage to take command of his goal area whether it be challenging an attacker for a high-lofted cross or diving to stop the point-blank shot of a goal-hungry forward. Whatever the case, the goalkeeper must be fearless in his defense of the goal.

A final quality required for successful goal tending is the ability to concentrate. Loss of concentration at any point during the game may result in a goal for the opposition. It is often difficult for the goalkeeper to concentrate on his job for the entire 90 minutes, especially in matches where he rarely touches the ball. However, he must discipline himself to be aware and alert at all times to make the game-winning save when it is required.

Even though a player may possess the essential components – quickness, anticipation, courage, and concentration – he must also develop the basic skills and techniques that will be used in actual game play.

Soccer

The basic W position for the goalkeeper's hands.

Low balls should be fielded with the fingers pointing downwards so that the ball can be scooped and trapped against the goalkeeper's chest.

Receiving the Ball

The goalkeeper prevents the opposition from scoring. To accomplish that objective, he must be sure-handed and able to receive a variety of different shots from the opposition. Generally speaking, the goalkeeper should try to hold on to any shot that he fields to prevent a second opportunity for hungry forwards to bang in a rebound. He must develop soft hands that will cushion and hold the most difficult shots.

The basic position for the hands is the W position, with the fingers extended and the thumb and forefinger of each hand touching. Balls coming above the waist should be fielded with the hands in the W position, hands pointing upward. However, balls that arrive below the waist should be fielded with the palms open and the fingers pointing downward. The keeper should always try to position his body in the flight path of the ball, in the event the ball slips through his hands. High, lofted balls coming into the goal area are usually the keeper's biggest problem. He must leap and catch the ball at the highest point possible to prevent opponents from heading in a score. Timing the jump correctly is essential when receiving high balls.

Punching the Ball

The goalkeeper may sometimes be forced to punch the ball away from his goal area, rather than try to make a difficult catch. If he decides to punch the ball, he should concentrate on directing the ball high, wide, and as far downfield as possible. The ball must be punched away from the area in front of the goal. The keeper may use one or both hands, depending on the situation. A one-handed punch is used to continue the flight of the ball on its original course. For instance, a ball crossed from the left side would be propelled in the same direction it was traveling. If the keeper wishes to change the direction of flight, a two-fisted punch should be employed, in which the clenched fists should be held together forming a solid surface with which to strike the ball. The movement of the arms should be a short, concentrated stroke. The sudden extension of the elbows will provide the needed power to propel the ball away from the threatened area.

Reducing the Angle

The soccer goal provides a large target and poses a problem for netminders as they endeavor to cover all sections of the goal. If the keeper can reduce the available space from which the opposition is shooting, his job will be easier. By moving out (forward) from the goal line, he can narrow the angle between himself and the ball, thus reducing the area that he is required to protect. There is a slight risk involved in moving out since the keeper may become vulnerable to the lob or chip shot over his head. However, it is very difficult to loft a chip shot accurately behind the keeper while under match pressure. Even so, he must exercise good judgment in determining how far to come out of the goal area.

Diving

In certain instances, *every goalkeeper must dive for the ball to make a save.* Acrobatic dives are as exciting as they are necessary for a good netminder. However, diving should never be used just as a crowd pleaser. Inexcusable mistakes sometimes occur when unnecessary, *eye-catching acrobatics replace sound goalkeeping tactics.*

When diving to make a save, do not dive either headfirst or feetfirst at the opponent since this provides cover for only a small portion of the goal. Instead, position the body to cover as much of the goal as possible. By obstructing as much of the opponent's shooting angle as possible, the goalkeeper will greatly increase his chances of a successful save.

Distribution

When the goalkeeper has made the initial save, his job is only half completed. He must then return the ball to a teammate for an effective counterattack. There are two basic methods of distributing the ball.

Throwing. The best method of distribution is throwing the ball. A goalkeeper who can accurately distribute a ball to his teammate has a decided advantage over the keeper who merely kicks the ball as far as possible downfield. When throwing, it is advantageous to direct the ball to a teammate's feet where he may gain quick control to initiate the attack.

Kicking. Most people kick or punt a soccer ball farther than they can throw it. Many

coaches will instruct their goalkeeper to distribute the ball by a long volley (punt) into the opponent's territory. This is an effective method of quickly playing the ball into the opposite end of the field, but it usually lacks the accuracy of a well-placed throw. Even so, the volley can sometimes be useful as a method of quick counterattack.

Soccer

Goalkeeper as a Defender
The keeper may picture himself as an extra defender; actually, he should fulfill that role. Support in the open space behind the defending fullback line is an essential function of the goalkeeper. He must anticipate penetrating passes into vulnerable space and be ready to leave his goal to outrace opposing forwards to the ball. The keeper working in unison with his defenders creates a defensive side that is hard to penetrate.

Directing the Defense
Since the goalkeeper is the last line of defense, he is in excellent position to view the play. He should use his position as an advantage, verbally directing his teammates in their defensive or attacking efforts. Excessive chatter is not desirable, but constructive comments are a plus for any team.

Defenders

Forming a line of defense in front of the goalkeeper are the defenders, or fullbacks. Most of the modern formations consist of a four-man fullback line, employing two central defenders flanked by right and left defenders. One of the central fullbacks is usually designated as a sweeper who supports the other three defenders. The other central defender plays as a stopper who challenges opponents in his area, often marking the opposing center forward. The wing defenders guard the opposing wingmen. Most teams attempt to free their sweeper from man-to-man marking so he can roam behind the defense, much like the free safety role in American football.

All great teams are based on a strong, technically sound defense. Defense is the name of the game at the highest levels of play. High-scoring games are rare in world-class soccer. This may well be one of the reasons soccer has not established itself as a major sport in America until recently. The popular sports of baseball, football, and basketball all involve more scoring per game than the average soccer match. The American public has adopted these sports and, as a result, many people find the transition to low-scoring soccer matches a change. Soccer might enjoy greater popularity in the States if goal scoring were increased. This theory seems to be supported by the widespread interest in indoor soccer, which produces more scoring, somewhat comparable to professional ice hockey. In conventional soccer, present rules, coupled with improvements in team tactics and sophisticated defensive concepts, make goal-scoring difficult.

In the past, the responsibilities of a defender differed significantly from the role he plays today. He was expected to do just what his title stated: defend. Total emphasis was placed upon destroying the opponent's attack, while little importance was given to initiating counterattacks. "Don't let the other team score and you've done your job" characterized defensive tactics

Courtesy New York Cosmos.

in the early years of the sport. Philosophies change, however. Modern systems require defenders to be complete players, defensively as well as offensively. When the goal has been successfully defended, the job is only halfway completed; now he must contribute to the attack.

Franz Beckenbauer is a prime example of a world-class defender who possesses excellent attacking ability. Timely runs forward to support the attackers put added pressure on the opposition and often result in a score. Beckenbauer's method of play exemplifies the modern tactical concept of total soccer, in which players both attack and defend. Great defenders possess certain qualities that allow them to excel. They must be strong, both on the ground and when challenging to win a ball in the air. They must be tenacious tacklers. Quickness and speed are definite advantages, although there are great defenders who are not blessed with outstanding speed. Anticipation and knowledge of the game sometimes compensate for a slight lack of speed. Coolness under game pressure – the ability to maintain composure – is the final characteristic associated with top-quality defenders. If a player can combine these qualities with basic technical knowledge of defensive concepts, he will become a definite asset to his team.

Winning Air Balls

Defenders must be a dominant force in the air. The ability to outjump opponents and win the air balls is an absolute requirement, especially against teams who tend to play long, lofted passes into the goal area. Wherever possible, defending players should head the ball to a teammate who can initiate a counterattack. However, when attempting a clearance in a crowd of players, it is wise to head the ball away from the goal even if it means directing it to an open space. The basic rule to be followed for the clearance header is to drive the ball high, wide, and as far from the goal as possible. A mistake in front of the net can easily result in an opponent's score, so the ball should be sent away from the area where most scoring chances originate.

Tackling

The act of challenging an opponent when he has possession of the ball is termed tackling. Every defender must work hard to become a capable tackler. When a decision to tackle has been made, it must be performed without hesitation. Half-hearted attempts, usually the result of indecision, must be avoided since they invariably leave the defender beaten and out of position. Tackles must be clean and hard with determination to win the ball. Determination will often compensate for a slight lack of physical, or technical, ability.

The most common method of tackling is the block tackle. As the defending player challenges his opponent, he blocks the ball, using the inside portion of the foot. Another method is the slide tackle. The defender executes the tackle by sliding into the ball and dislodging it from his opponent. The slide tackle should be used sparingly, since the defender must leave his feet.

Use the inside of the foot to block tackle the ball.

A final technique is the poke tackle. As the name suggests, the defender uses his toe to poke the ball away from his opponent.

When tackling, it is important not to commit yourself too early or signal the intent to your opponent. Since the opponent will be using body feints, the defender must react to small cues that might reveal the opponent's next move.

Shoulder Charge

The laws governing play prohibit violent physical contact. However, a limited amount of body contact is legal when two opposing players are challenging each other for the ball. The

The slide tackle should be used sparingly. However, it is a successful method of dislodging the ball from an opponent.

shoulder charge is an effective technique to dislodge an opponent from the ball. The upper part of the shoulder moves an opponent away from the ball, or at least stops his momentum. The shoulder charge is permitted only when the ball is within playing distance of both players, usually 5 to 6 feet, and, in the referee's judgment, the player is attempting to play the ball, not the man.

Reading the Play

An important characteristic of quality defenders is their ability to anticipate the intentions of their opponents in advance. Thinking a split second ahead of their opposition, they always seem to be in position to intercept passes or break up an attack. It is not mere chance that top-flight defenders read the game so well; it is due to a combination of playing experience and serious study of the game. In addition to skill and tactics, intelligence and game sense play a vital role in successful defensive strategy.

Midfielders

The success or failure of almost every soccer team depends ultimately on its midfield play. Probably the most difficult of all positions, the midfielder is the link between defense and attack. He patrols a large section of the playing area, ranging from deep in his own defensive zone to the opponent's goal. As a result, he covers plenty of ground during the game and must be able to perform under heavy physical strain. Good midfielders must be efficient at distributing the ball

Courtesy Tampa Bay Rowdies. Photo by Steinmetz.

and must know how to adjust the firmness and type of pass for various situations. The ability to move forward and attack the goal when the opportunity arises is an added benefit. Attacking midfielders create added pressure on the opposition and often open scoring opportunities for their own forwards. Since most attacking maneuvers originate in the middle sector of the field, a team that lacks effective midfield build-up usually has problems scoring goals.

Pelé, probably the greatest soccer player ever, is an excellent example of an attacking midfielder. Although occupying an inside forward position during most of his Brazilian soccer career, he splendidly accepted the role of midfielder while with the New York Cosmos of the NASL. Supporting the front running forwards, he still scored goals at an amazing rate while directing play from his central position.

Many international teams seem to be built around great midfield players who dictate the tempo and the style of play for their respective teams. Midfielders must develop a high level of skill to excel at their position. In addition, tactical game sense and peak physical condition are attributes that separate top-flight players from the lesser ones.

Positional Play

Many players seem to run endlessly during the entire 90 minutes of a match without achieving positive results. They always seem to be one step behind the ball, forever chasing it to all corners of the field. It is the absence of correct positional play by the midfielders that usually results in partial or complete breakdown of the team's tactical system. It is not the midfielder's role to run unrestricted whenever and wherever he desires. He is the link that connects defenders with attackers and must serve in that function if the team is to succeed. Intelligent movement, with or without the ball, is essential, creating space and opportunities for teammates. After a game is analyzed, it is usually discovered that it was won or lost in the middle of the field. Thus, a great deal of responsibility rests upon the midfielders for the role they fulfill in the field.

Fitness of the Midfield Player

The midfielder runs longer and harder than the other players. Although every soccer player must be conditioned to play with great physical intensity while performing the necessary tasks with skill, the midfield player must be at peak physical condition to perform efficiently. Players who are not physically fit usually discover that their skills diminish markedly as the game progresses. In order to remain at a high technique level for the entire game, the midfielder must be well prepared, both physically and mentally. There is no substitute for proper fitness, although many players try to convince themselves that they can still contribute their best efforts while not in peak physical condition.

Courtesy Philadelphia Fury. Photo by Tom Guidotti.

Soccer

Courtesy New York Cosmos.

Composure under Pressure

Whether pressure is caused by an opponent's efforts or by a clock ticking off the final minutes, a midfielder must not lose composure under the stress of adversity. He must not panic or resort to tactics that make him a poorer player. Changing the style of play based solely on the time remaining in the game is a foolish gesture. Kicking the ball as far and as fast as possible is not a timesaver for the player or the team. The chances of losing ball possession are greatly increased with that type of play. It is much wiser to play basic, composed soccer whether it be in the first or the last few minutes of play. Chances of success are at a maximum if midfielders perform with high playing standards during pressure situations.

Courtesy Tulsa Roughnecks.

Soccer

Forwards – Strikers and Wingers

The greatest thrill in soccer is scoring an important goal. Thousands of players have dreamed of the moment that they become the hero of the game by smashing the ball against the back of the net while listening to the roar of the crowd as they receive the congratulations of teammates. For this reason, the forward line tends to be the favorite position of many young players. The vision of becoming another Pelé or Gerd Mueller convinces them that the forward line is where it's happening.

A goal-scoring forward does receive a fair share of publicity, and rightly so. Consistently putting the ball in the back of the net is the most difficult task in soccer. With the development of today's sophisticated defenses and the low scoring associated with most professional games, the forward who can finish an attack with a goal is a very important commodity.

The wingers, or outside forwards, operate on the flanks of the attack, attempting to draw opponents away from central defensive positions. Wingmen create space and scoring opportunities for their teammates through intelligent running and the ability to penetrate the opposing defense. They also initiate many attacks by withdrawing into their own half of the field to receive outlet passes from their goalkeeper or defensemen. Defensively, the wingers usually mark the opposing wing fullbacks making overlap runs and may withdraw to defend against opposition kickoffs.

The center forward, or central striker, spearheads the attack and is considered the team's primary goal scorer. He must be an opportunist at creating goals out of half chances and defensive mistakes. Since the striker is tightly marked, he must be able to perform skillfully under heavy pressure. Defensively, he must challenge for possession of the ball in the central, attacking third of the field, hoping to force mistakes by the opposition thereby creating scoring opportunities for his team.

It is difficult to pinpoint the reasons why one player may develop into a dominant forward while another, with seemingly equal ability, never quite achieves his full potential. The great attackers have the physical and emotional make-up that enables them to succeed at their profession, while others with equal talent fail. The following qualities are important factors influencing successful attacking play.

Strength on the Ball

A forward's job is to score. An attacker must protect his possession of the ball and must be prepared for the hard knocks that will invariably occur. Since one cannot score unless the ball is under control, every player should strive not to relinquish possession until he passes to a teammate or shoots on goal.

Courtesy Tampa Bay Rowdies. Photo by Steinmetz.

Soccer

Control under Pressure from an Opponent

The ability to receive a ball properly is essential for every player. Whether it be taking the pace off a ball played to the feet, receiving a high-lob pass on the chest, or settling a bouncing ball with the thigh, good forwards must be able to receive and control a pass quickly. Since most attackers are tightly marked by defenders, these ball skills must be performed in pressure situations. While practicing, arrange game situations involving opponents and become accustomed to simulated game pressure.

Shooting Ability

Forwards must be able to release their shots quickly in varying situations that occur in a match, whether falling, turning, or twisting. The ability to shoot without setting up the ball is a must. The ball always attracts a crowd, so forwards will not have a great deal of time or space in which to operate. Quick reactions during pressure situations result in goals, just as slow or indecisive movements result in loss of possession. Every forward must develop the ability to shoot equally well with both feet. Many players consistently use only their strongest foot and are predictable in their play. Scoring chances have been wasted because the ball was first tapped to the stronger foot before the shot was attempted. Learn to use both feet and you will be on your way to becoming a complete soccer player.

Determination

Good forwards are blessed with more than outstanding physical ability. Attitude and emotional make-up are often deciding factors in distinguishing the great from the average player. Determination to succeed, regardless of circumstances, is a quality virtually impossible to instill in a player. It must originate from within. The ability to overcome adversity and not lose heart enables a player to bounce back when things go wrong. Maintaining a consistency in play is essential to successful soccer.

Confidence

Confidence in one's own ability is very important if a player is to reach his full potential. True confidence enables the player to relax while participating in the match and allows maximum functioning of physical and mental skills. Confidence does not mean being arrogant or underestimating your opponent. It merely indicates awareness of capabilities and faith in oneself to contribute whatever is necessary to the team effort. Total belief in oneself results in outstanding player performance.

Courtesy Philadelphia Fury. Photo by Mike Levin.

Soccer

Courtesy New York Cosmos.

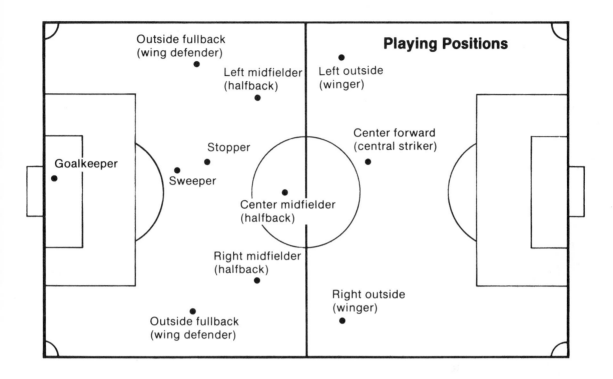

Playing Positions

Outside fullback (wing defender)

Left midfielder (halfback)

Left outside (winger)

Center forward (central striker)

Stopper

Goalkeeper

Sweeper

Center midfielder (halfback)

Right midfielder (halfback)

Right outside (winger)

Outside fullback (wing defender)

Although goal-scoring forwards receive accolades for their achievements, it is important to realize that they have not amassed impressive records without help. Team play usually leads to success, while the solo efforts of the individual may prove futile. Many players do not score with consistency, yet play a vital role in the goal-scoring process. Defenders who initiate the attack with accurate passes, midfielders who link the defense with the attack, and wingers who draw opponents out of position and slip the ball to the center forward waiting to drive it home are just as important to successful play as the team member who scores. Assisting on a goal can be as satisfying as notching a tally. Always remember to place team welfare above any desire for fame or personal glory. Forwards cannot be selfish and still contribute significantly to the total team effort. When the opportunity to score presents itself, do not hesitate to take it. If it doesn't materialize, do not force the situation; rather, give the ball to a teammate who may be in a better position to finish the play. A goal scored, regardless of which player tallies, is the ultimate purpose of the team effort.

Courtesy Houston Hurricane. Photo by Mark Burns.

4.Techniques of Field Play

The old saying that practice makes perfect is true when speaking about soccer. Not only should a player be fit both physically and mentally, but he must also master the basic technical skills that are necessary for advanced levels of play. Skills such as passing, shooting, and receiving balls can be acquired only through diligent practice. There are no shortcuts to becoming a good player. Stars such as Johann Cruyff and Franz Beckenbauer did not simply walk on the field and excel. Their high standard of play is the result of hours of practice in the basics. Even after gaining recognition as international-class players, they must continue to maintain an advanced level of skill through constant practice of fundamentals.

For young players, it is especially important to constantly strive to improve their skill and technical ability in passing, receiving, heading, shooting, dribbling, screening, and feinting. Remember, the only way to develop a high standard of play is hard work.

Passing

In order to blend eleven individuals into a functioning team, each player must know the techniques used in passing. Inaccurate passing is the swiftest, surest way of destroying the vital teamwork necessary for successful soccer. Each player must know the various methods of passing the ball as well as when and where to pass it. Many players hold the ball too long and place themselves in situations that limit their passing options. An attacking player should possess the ball just long enough to draw an opponent out of position, which consequently allows an attacking teammate open space. At that moment, a well-timed pass to the open man is desirable. Such a pass will put the attacking team in a numerical advantage over the defending team in that section of the field. It is reasonable to assume that a team's chance of success will be greater if it can create two-on-one or three-on-one situations.

When passing there are several basic guidelines to follow:

Be accurate. Concentration is necessary to ensure an accurate pass. A misdirected pass is worse than no pass at all.

Play positive. When possible, the ball should be played forward. The penetrating pass creates problems for a defensive unit and places the attacking side in a better position to score. Passing the ball back to a supporting teammate should be used to set up a penetrating pass or as an outlet when no positive options present themselves. Square passing (i.e., passing flat across the field) is considered dangerous because of a high

Courtesy Ft. Lauderdale Strikers. Photo by Barton L. Gilmore.

likelihood of interception. That type of pass must be used sparingly and carefully. Too much square passing may result in a slow attacking buildup, which allows the defense extra time to recover.

Execute properly. Depending on the situation, each player must learn to adjust the pace (velocity) of the pass. In some cases, the ball must be firmly played to a teammate's feet, while in another instance a softer, more delicate pass is required. A split-second decision is needed for proper execution.

Watch the ball. At the moment the pass is initiated, a player should have his eyes squarely on the ball. Eye-foot coordination is essential if mistakes are to be avoided. This is not to say that a player should always have his head down while moving the ball. The head should be kept up, enabling the player to see what is happening around him. However, at the moment of contact with the ball, the passer's vision must be concentrated on the point of impact.

Methods and Technique

Many different forms of passing can be spotted in a soccer match. Passes struck with the instep, those directed by the outside of the foot, and chips over defenders are only a few of the possibilities. The following is a list of the basic passing techniques.

Inside-of-the-foot pass. The pass most often used in American soccer, it is often performed incorrectly. Four basic rules must be followed to ensure effective passing technique. First, lock the ankle. The kicking foot must have the ankle locked with the toes pointing up and away from the midline of the body. Locking the ankle provides a solid surface with which to strike the ball. Second, point the nonkicking foot toward the intended target. This will improve the accuracy of the pass. Third, do not swing the entire leg when striking the ball. With the knee acting as a hinge, only the lower leg should be utilized in the kicking process. This method allows the player more stability when passing. Finally, follow through with a kicking motion. This is absolutely necessary for any well-struck pass.

Outside-of-the-foot pass. The outside portion of the foot is also used to pass the ball. The foot should be extended forward and slightly inward. The ball is then struck with the outer section of the foot, which causes the ball to curve in flight due to the reverse spin motion. With this type of pass, the nonkicking foot should be pointed in the direction the player is facing, not in the direction the pass is traveling.

The Brazilians have developed excellent passing skills using the outside of the foot. They have the ability to swerve passes around defenders to waiting teammates. At the present time, this type of pass is not well developed among most American players.

Inside-of-the-foot pass.

Outside-of-the-foot pass.

Instep pass.

Instep pass. The instep, often used to strike the ball when shooting, is also used for passing. It is the area of the foot covered by the laces of the shoe. When match situation dictates the need of a long, firmly driven pass for a quick counterattack, the side of the foot is inadequate since it does not generate enough power. Using the instep, a player can powerfully direct medium- and long-range passes to teammates. Keep the pass on the ground if possible; it is much easier to control a pass on the ground than one in the air.

Chip pass. During a match, a player may sometimes find a defender positioned between himself and a teammate. If proper technique is applied, he can chip the ball over the defender. To do that, drive the foot under the ball with a short, powerful motion of the leg. In doing so the pass will be lifted up and over the opponent. A well-placed chip will leave the defender beaten and out of position. Goals have also been tallied by clever forwards who can lob shots over the outstretched arms of a goalkeeper. Certain professional players are very adept at chip shots and have scored seemingly impossible goals.

Chest pass. Pelé, an expert at every phase of the game, occasionally used his chest to pass the ball. This type of pass is uncommon to most players, but it can be very deceptive. A quick turn of the upper body as the ball strikes the chest will result in the pass rebounding off the chest in the desired direction. This is an excellent method of one-touch passing and is especially useful in situations where the passing player is tightly marked by a defender.

Drills to improve passing technique
- One- and two-touch passing with a partner over short distances.
- Stationary interpassing over varying distances to a target.
- Interpassing with a teammate while jogging slowly.
- Volleying a ball to both stationary and moving targets.
- Half-volleying a ball to both stationary and moving targets.
- Chip passes over the head of one teammate to another teammate.
- Chip passes to a moving teammate.
- Form a triangle with two other players, about 10-15 yards apart. Pass the ball to another player in the triangle who receives it with one foot and passes it with the opposite foot to another player.
- Six players form a circle around a central player with the ball. The central player passes the ball to someone on the perimeter and then switches positions with that person, who in turn passes to another player on the perimeter of the circle. The drill stresses continuous passing and interchanging of positions.

Inside-of-the-foot trap.

Outside-of-the-foot trap.

Practice hints
- Practice first with a stationary ball, then progress to a moving ball as passing skills improve.
- The ankle must be firm when you attempt to pass the ball. Otherwise, you will lose both power and accuracy in your passing.
- Keep your eye on the ball at the moment you intend to pass it.
- Learn to pass the ball equally well with either foot.
- Practice varying the pace of your passes.

Receiving

The ability to control a moving ball is essential, whether playing at the amateur or professional level. Since the ball will arrive in a number of different ways, the player must learn to receive the ball with any part of his body except the hands or arms. Receiving a ball traveling at high speed is a skill that can only be acquired through constant repetition. A ball should be included in all training drills, even those designed primarily for fitness, so players will develop the touch necessary for good ball control.

Thigh trap.

Chest trap.

A common mistake many players make when receiving a pass is bringing the ball to a complete stop. Once the ball is dead, the player must restart it in the direction he intends to move. The stopping and subsequent restarting of the ball require extra moments that can be crucial in advanced levels of play. It is much more effective if the player receiving the ball does not completely stop it but gives it a nudge in the direction of his next movement. Precious moments will be conserved, which may be the difference between success and disappointment.

Inside-of-the-foot trap. Basically the same form is used in receiving a ball as in passing. However, when receiving, the foot must act as a cushion as the ball arrives. Relaxing the leg at the moment of contact will achieve the cushioning effect. The receiving foot should reach out to meet the ball and, as the ball is touched, should be withdrawn. Such motion will take the pace off the ball.

Outside-of-the-foot trap. A pass directed toward you from the side is often received with the outside portion of the foot. This may also be an effective means of screening an opponent if the body is correctly positioned between him and the ball.

Sole-of-the-foot trap. A very simple way of controlling the ball, this method is rarely used unless the ball is coming directly at a player. The receiving foot should be elevated off the ground with the toes pointing upward. The ball is trapped between the sole of the foot and the ground. The opposite leg should be slightly bent for flexibility.

Thigh trap. The thigh is often used in controlling a ball that is dropping from the air. As the ball makes contact, the thigh should be slightly withdrawn to cushion the ball and drop it at the feet of the player.

Chest trap. For many players, the most difficult passes to receive and control are those that arrive at chest level. Even so, the complete player should master the technique of receiving that sort of pass. At the moment of impact, the chest must be drawn concavely inward. If proper timing is achieved, the ball will bounce slightly off the chest and drop to the ground.

Head trap. This method of control is seldom observed except at the highest levels of play. Most players think only of heading a ball away, but with practice it can be controlled. Execution of the head trap requires almost perfect timing with very little margin for error. The secret is that the player must jump early and meet the ball as he is beginning to descend. Since he is traveling downward as the ball arrives, it is cushioned and will not bounce away as would a normally headed ball. Jumping too late destroys the timing and results in the ball rebounding away, out of control.

Drills to improve trapping technique
- Stand facing a teammate, about 5 yards apart. Roll a ball to your teammate who receives it using any surface of the foot – inside, outside, instep, or sole – and then gives you a return pass. Repeat for 1 minute, then switch positions.
- Stand facing a teammate, about 10 yards apart. Lob a ball so it drops at the thigh, chest, or head level. The teammate receives the ball, brings it under control, and returns it to you. Repeat for 1 minute, then switch positions.
- Receive balls traveling at various speeds and heights while running.
- Control a variety of passes while under pressure of an opponent.
- Organize small-sided games emphasizing ball control.

Practice hints
- Learn to receive and control the ball with both feet.
- Relax the part of the body in contact with the ball to create a cushioning effect.
- Concentrate on watching the ball as it arrives.
- Once the ball is controlled, accurately pass it to a designated target.

Jump early to meet the ball. At contact, move the head backward to cushion the ball and bring it under control.

Heading

Soccer is the only major professional sport in which the head is commonly used to strike the ball. Heading is a skill that many players seem to overlook, possibly due to the lack of emphasis placed upon it by many of our youth coaches. It is a misconceived notion that a player must only out-leap his opponent to accomplish his task. That is the same as saying all a player has to do is kick the ball to fulfill a useful function. The head can be used to perform the basic skills of passing, trapping, and shooting. The forehead provides a flat surface for striking the ball and aids in accurately directing the ball to a target. When leaping, the back should be arched, the neck rigid, and the chin tucked in toward the chest. As the ball makes contact with the forehead, the upper body is snapped forward. Proper timing of that motion provides power to the head-driven ball.

Methods and Technique

Passing with the head. When passing to a teammate, accuracy is paramount. A misdirected pass usually ends up in the possession of an opponent. The ball should be aimed downward to a teammate's feet where it can be easily controlled.

Scoring with the head. Many goals are scored by opportunistic forwards who have the ability and courage to win air battles. A big, strong center forward can cause many problems if he dominates air balls in the opponent's goal area. Many great goal scorers, notably Geoff Hurst and Pelé, have been outstanding headers. Players who possess the skill coupled with determination to win air balls are valuable assets to any team.

Courtesy Dallas Tornado.

When attempting to score, be sure to direct the ball on a downward angle toward the goal line. It is much more difficult for a goalkeeper to handle low shots than those coming above the waist. Forwards attempting to drive powerful headers past the goalkeeper should realize that deflections that quickly change the flight path of the ball can be most effective.

Defensive heading. A defender heading the ball should, if possible, direct a pass out of danger to one of his teammates. Certain situations may make this procedure unsafe, especially if the play is in the immediate goal area with an aggressive center forward nearby. In that case the ball should be cleared up and away. Never head a ball downward in an area where a waiting opponent can volley it into the net.

Drills to improve heading technique
- Standing 5 yards apart, lob balls to your teammate who heads them back to you. Repeat for 1 minute, then switch positions.

Soccer

Courtesy New York Cosmos.

- Slowly jog forward while heading a ball served by a teammate. Repeat jogging backward.
- Your teammate serves high cross passes into the goal area. Time your run, jump, and head for goal.
- Playing as a defender, practice clearance headers as your teammate serves cross passes into the goal area.
- Practice the dive header as your partner serves low balls (waist height).

Practice hints
- Contact the ball on your forehead.
- Keep your eyes open and on the ball as you head it.
- Keep your mouth closed when heading to avoid accidentally biting your tongue.
- Don't wait for the ball to strike your head; meet it.
- Arch your back from the waist and, as the ball arrives, snap forward to generate power.
- When jumping to head the ball, timing is critical. Try to jump early and hang in the air, meeting the ball at your highest point.

Shooting

Many players agree the most enjoyable portion of a practice session is shooting at the goal. Everyone, save the goalkeeper, likes to see the goal net recoil with the impact of a well-timed shot. Forwards dream of a blistering shot that no goalkeeper could possibly stop, and many defenders visualize themselves notching an important tally to the delight of the crowd. It is especially important that each player, regardless of position, develop adequate shooting skills. The ability to shoot powerfully and accurately can be acquired by all if the correct techniques are applied.

It is not mere coincidence that some players possess a deadly shot while others just can't seem to strike the ball well. If the shooting motion is broken down into its component parts, certain rules can be developed that, if followed, will aid in improving shooting skills.

Head down. When shooting, the head must be pointed downwardnand vision concentrated on the point of impact. Such form ensures eye-to-ball coordination.

Kicking foot extended. Extension of the kicking foot results in the toes pointing downward as the ball is contacted. This form will help to achieve the desired low shot.

Nonkicking foot. The positioning of the nonkicking foot is very important. As the shot is taken, the nonkicking foot should be planted beside the ball, ensuring that the player's body leans over the ball. Placing the foot behind the ball results in the body leaning slightly backward, which increases the possibility of raising the shot, often over the goal.

Follow-through. Whether hitting a baseball or kicking a soccer ball, follow-through is important in providing power and distance.

Every team should include a variety of shooting drills during practice sessions. The game dictates that a player must have the ability to release his shot quickly and accurately, so training should be designed with that in mind. The construction of a kickwall provides a good surface at which individuals can shoot and follow up rebounds. Whatever the method used, players at all levels must develop and maintain shooting proficiency.

Methods and Technique

Instep drive. Shooting with the instep requires a strong follow-through of the kicking leg. As the ball is struck, the nonkicking foot should be planted directly beside the ball and pointed in the direction you want the ball to travel. This method generates powerful shots with the potential of scoring from outside the penalty area.

Banana shot. The ball can curve in flight if proper spin is applied. This shot is called the banana shot. It can be a very effective attacking skill since it is difficult for the keeper to judge the flight of the ball correctly. To ensure sufficient spin, the ball must be struck along its outer perimeter. Using the inside of the right foot on the right side of the ball will cause counterclockwise rotation and curve the shot to the left. If the outside of the right foot is impacted on the left side of the ball, a clockwise spin results in a curve to the right. The opposite is true of a left-footed kick. Either method, if performed correctly, generates the banana-like flight of the ball.

Instep drive. Place the nonkicking foot directly beside the ball.　Strike the ball with the laces of the shoe.

The banana shot is especially effective on direct or indirect free kicks. The defending team will usually position a wall of men in front of the goal to prevent a kicker from having a direct line to the entire goal width. A well-executed banana shot will curve around the wall and make it difficult for the keeper to defend since he is being screened by his own teammates. Rivelino, the great midfielder from Brazil, is one of the best at bending free kicks around a defensive wall.

Half volley. If a ball dropping from the air is struck just as it hits the ground, the resulting shot is termed the half volley. Timing is very critical, since striking the ball even a fraction of a second late will result in an inaccurate shot. If it is well-timed, tremendous power can be generated.

Volley. Sometimes a shot must be attempted with a bouncing ball. It can be very difficult to keep a shot of that type in a low trajectory. The ball is often driven high and far over the goal. It is very important to kick down through the ball, ideally by getting the knee of the kicking leg over the ball as it is struck. This can be accomplished by leaping to a position slightly higher than the bouncing ball or by swinging the kicking leg horizontal to the ground. If that position is attained, there is little possibility of the shot sailing high.

Powerful follow through of the kicking leg.

Soccer

Bicycle kick. The most acrobatic of all shots is the bicycle kick. It derives its name from the scissor-like motion of the legs when striking the ball. The bicycle kick is used when attempting to shoot a ball that is traveling above your head. You must leap, throwing your legs up and over the head, and with a bicycle-like motion shoot the ball. If proper form is attained, it will actually look similar to peddling a bike upside down. Needless to say, this type of shot is very difficult to complete successfully and should be used only in favorable situations. If the attempt is made, care must be taken to cushion the fall with the hands; otherwise, the kicker may injure himself. Often a player is intent on making the shot, forgets to break his fall, and ends up landing on his neck or head. Have two persons present when practicing this type of shot. The partner can help cushion the fall until the correct technique is developed.

Penalty shot. The penalty shot is strictly a one-on-one situation: the kicker and the goalkeeper. The ball is placed on a spot 12 yards directly in front of the goal. A basic rule that all players should follow is that they decide in advance which corner of the goal to shoot at when the whistle is blown. Most penalty kicks that are missed are due to indecisiveness on the part of the kicker. Pick a corner, have confidence, and let it fly.

Drills to improve your shooting technique
- Shoot stationary balls placed at various spots in the penalty area.
- Pass to a teammate, receive a return pass, and shoot at the goal.
- Volley and half-volley shooting at goal.
- Starting 40 yards from goal, dribble at top speed towards the goal and shoot.
- Control long, cross passes from a teammate and shoot at the goal.
- First-time shooting of passes arriving from various directions and distances.
- Shooting while being pressured by an opponent.
- Bending or curving stationary balls around an obstacle into the goal.

Practice hints
- Keep your head down and your eye on the ball as you kick it.
- Don't lean back as you shoot; lean over the ball.
- Develop the ability to shoot first-time.
- Concentrate on accuracy as well as power.
- Practice shooting with both feet.
- Aim your shots low and to the corners of the goal; these are the most difficult for a goalkeeper to save.

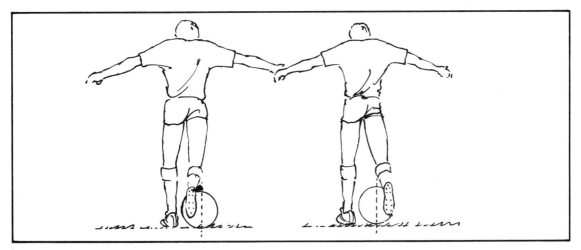

Bending (banana) shots. Striking a ball with the right foot on the inside of the center will cause it to bend to the right. Striking a ball on the outside of center will cause it to curve to the left.

Dribbling

Certain players have the ability to thrill the crowd with spectacular dribbling skills. They use clever body feints while running with the ball and leave flat-footed, astonished defenders behind them. George Best, the controversial Irish star, was probably one of the best in the world at taking on an opponent. On occasion, he has dribbled through an entire team to score unbelievable goals. For most of us, though, excessive dribbling results in loss of possession. Disruption of overall team play will result if dribbling is not constructive. All players must realize that dribbling is a beneficial part of the game only if used in the proper situations.

Probably the most disliked member of any squad is the ball hog who won't pass the ball once he acquires it. The ball hog tries to dribble past any or all defenders who confront him, never thinking of passing off as an alternative to losing possession. His behavior angers teammates and hurts the overall team effort. In his case, the art of dribbling has been abused and misused. The intelligent player will use dribbling as it is warranted. It is tactically wise to dribble straight toward an opponent, forcing him to confront the dribbler. The ball is then passed to an open teammate. Drawing the defender out of position serves the fundamental purpose of creating open space in the defense. However, all efforts will be wasted if the ball is held longer than necessary. Combining dribbling skills with intelligent passing can destroy a defense. Excessive dribbling only creates problems for the attacking team and gives the defense an easy day's work.

Soccer

The technique of dribbling is not easily explained since there really isn't any definite style. Each player uses different methods of beating an opponent. Head and body feints, false stops, or sudden changes in direction are all part of the technique. What works with one player might not fit the style of another. We must all develop our own particular variations. It can be helpful to watch professional games to acquire new ideas.

All players must practice dribbling just as they would any other soccer skill since it is an integral part of team play. It is a very individualistic skill and can be practiced either with teammates or alone. Intelligent dribbling can be as exciting as it is beneficial; however, indiscriminate dribbling has no useful function.

Drills to improve dribbling technique
- Jog with the ball, nudging it along with the insides of both feet.
- Jog with the ball, using only the outside and instep surfaces of both feet.
- While dribbling, follow a moving teammate who is also dribbling the ball.
- Set up a series of cones, 3-5 yards apart. Dribble in and out of the cones at top speed while keeping the ball under close control.
- Dribble among a crowd of teammates in a restricted space, darting into open space while avoiding other players.

- In a restricted area, dribble and shield the ball from an opponent who is trying to gain possession.
- Dribble at and take on a defender while going toward a goal.

Practice hints
- Use all surfaces of the foot – inside, instep, and outside.
- When dribbling keep your head up as much as possible; don't look down at the ball except at the moment you contact it.
- Be deceptive; change speed and direction when dribbling.
- Keep the ball under control, close to your feet where it is protected from opponents.
- Develop dribbling ability with both feet.

Screening

A skill that is often overlooked or entirely omitted in training sessions is the art of screening, or shielding, the ball. Every player must learn the correct method of protecting the ball when tightly marked by an opponent. Positioning the body is all-important if one is to master the technique. For example, if a defender attempts to tackle the ball from an opponent's left side, the player in possession should control the ball with his right foot and position his body between the defender and the ball. Likewise, if the defender tackles from the right side, his opponent should control the ball with his left foot. If correctly screened, it will be almost impossible for the defender to steal the ball unless he fouls the man in possession.

> *Drills to improve screening technique*
> * Protect the ball from a teammate who attempts to gain possession in a restricted area.

Courtesy Tampa Bay Rowdies. Photo by Steinmetz.

- Receive a pass while under pressure of an opponent. Shield the ball until a support player arrives.
- Place 8-10 players, each with a ball, inside the center circle. All players dribble and protect their ball while attempting to kick their opponent's ball out of the area.

Practice hints
- Always position your body between the opponent and the ball.
- Keep your head up; know where your opponent is so you can move accordingly.
- Learn to use both feet when screening the ball.
- Be prepared to pass to a teammate should the opportunity arise.

Feints

Body feints are movements designed to deceive an opponent. The intent is to throw the opponent off-balance, causing him to move in the wrong direction. The feinting movement may be a dip of the shoulder, a quick turn of the head, or any other motion that confuses the opposition. Attackers, when dribbling, often use feinting movement to elude defenders. However, body feints are also used by defenders. When confronting an opponent who is in possession of the ball, defending players use feints to cause a premature, hurried move by the attacker. These deceptive movements, performed with or without the ball, are important skills that must be perfected by all players.

Drills to improve feinting technique
- While dribbling, practice a variety of feinting movements without opposition.
- With a teammate, practice feints while dribbling toward one another.

Practice hints
- Begin with basic feints and progress to more difficult ones as your skill level improves.
- Develop feinting moves to both your right and left.
- Constant repetition against an opponent will perfect your deception.

Mastering the basic skills needed to play the game takes work. Each player must be willing to devote a great deal of time and effort to acquire the fundamentals. Beginners may

have difficulty as they attempt to control the ball with movements and body positions never previously used. With continued practice, however, they will gradually feel more comfortable and skill levels will increase. It is advisable to practice skills in a progressive pattern, initially learning the most basic skills and gradually progressing to more difficult techniques. Initial practice should stress proper execution. Begin by walking through the motions and increase the speed of execution as you become more confident. Ultimately you should be able to perform each skill under game conditions.

Practice periods should be well-organized, meaningful, and progressive. As skill level increases, small-sided games can be organized that emphasize particular skill performance. For instance, a possession game involving 4 players (2 vs. 2) could be conducted in the center circle. Restricted in space, each team attempts to keep the ball away from its opponent. Goals are scored if one team can link together 10 consecutive passes. Such games will provide practice on a variety of skills, including dribbling, shielding, and feinting moves, in a gamelike situation. They also teach teamwork, movement with and without the ball, and positional play. The element of competition encourages each player to work harder. Last but not least, these small, organizational games are fun. It is very important that practice does not become tedious and boring or players will lose their motivation. Training sessions can and should be enjoyable.

Once you have developed proficiency, do not become complacent. You must practice constantly to maintain skill. Continued, repetitive practice is the only way to become an outstanding player.

5.Defensive Tactics

Anyone who has played in game competition knows how difficult it is to score goals. The congratulations and back slapping that always follow a score give testimony to that fact. It is not mere coincidence that prolific goal getters are a rare species, and a fellow who can consistently put the ball in the net is indeed valuable. The defensive side, responsible for preventing goals, is dedicated to denying easy scores to the opposition. It is important to realize that solid defensive soccer is not only the result of great individual play but also of sound tactical concepts and teamwork. It has become a calculated science in which each player must realize his part in the total scheme of play. A team might have the best individual defenders, but if they do not function as a unit the defense will break down. Combining physical ability with intelligent tactical play is the only way to create an outstanding defensive side.

Every player automatically becomes a defender once his team loses possession of the ball. This is not to say that forwards should gallop backward into their own penalty area to defend, but it does mean that once possession has been lost, everyone must aid in regaining the ball. If an attacker believes that he is only required to play offensive soccer, he becomes a detriment to the defense. All must be prepared to assume defensive responsibilities. A general understanding of basic defensive concepts is required of all players, including the goalkeeper.

Zone Defense vs. Man-to-Man Defense

There have always been arguments about the relative merits of different systems, particularly zonal and man-to-man. When playing zone defense, each player is responsible for defending a specific area of the field. If an opponent enters a zone, he becomes the responsibility of the man assigned to defend that area. As the opponent leaves the zone, he becomes the responsibility of someone else. Man-to-man defense is exactly what the name implies. Each player is assigned an opponent to mark, regardless of where he might be on the field.

Choosing the most effective system is difficult since all systems have strong and weak points. One advantage of zonal defense is that it usually results in correct positional play since players are not easily drawn out of their respective areas. Critics argue that zonal defense permits too large an area in which opponents can maneuver. The area between zones is often a no-man's-land because defenders may be hesitant in tackling an opponent who is on the outer edge of their area. Flooding a specific zone with more than one attacker also causes problems since it puts the defender at a numerical disadvantage. The disadvantages outweigh the advantages in strict zonal defense.

Proponents of the man-to-man defensive concept emphasize its positive aspects. Since each player is assigned an opponent, all opposing players will be tightly marked. The chances of an opponent running free are less than in zonal defense due to the reduced available space. The concept of strict man-to-man defense is also easy to comprehend, it is the task of each player to mark his opponent wherever he goes. However, this method is not without its disadvantages. A team that can isolate a good individual forward on a less-talented player will have an easy time. A man-to-man defense can entice inexperienced players into poor defensive

positions. Teammates drawn out of position cause confusion among the remaining defenders, which can lead to disaster. In addition, some players, overly concerned with marking an opponent tightly, do not know when to leave their man and contribute to the attack. Strict man-to-man defense is not without its problems.

What is the answer? Which system is really more effective? Which method should your team use? It is obvious that a combination of both, utilizing the strongest aspects of each, is the best system. Most clubs are currently using the combined system. Each player must be aware of his positional responsibilities but must also realize that an opponent entering a critical area should be tightly guarded. The general rule is to play man-to-man defense in the immediate area of the ball while zoning on the side of the field away from the ball. Zoning away from the ball provides depth in defense.

Most coaches like to use one defender as a sweeper who is not responsible for any particular man but who plays a zonal role in defense. The defenders in front of him are usually assigned man-to-man coverage and understand that, if beaten, the sweeper will be supporting them as a second line of defense. Each team must decide which system is suitable, taking into account the capabilities of its players. The basic concepts of defense always remain the same, but a good coach will develop a system best adapted to his players.

Depth in Defense

Defending sides should never be caught in a position where a penetrating pass can beat the entire defense. To avoid such a situation, the defense should not position players in a straight line across the field. It is much wiser to create depth in defense so that each player is supported from behind by a teammate. When depth of defense is maintained, fast breaks by the opposition will be held to a minimum.

Concentrated Defense

Most goals are scored from a central location encompassing the area directly in front of the goal. Rarely does a shot taken on goal from the extreme wing positions result in a score. Wingers operating along the sidelines are encouraged to cross the ball to a central attacker with a better shooting angle. For that reason, consolidating defenders in the most dangerous scoring zones has become an accepted standard. Rather than positioning wing defenders out near the sidelines, which tends to spread out the defense, most teams now pull their wing defenders closer to the central defenders. This tactic allows opposing wing forwards more open space, but it limits the available space in the most dangerous scoring zone, especially in front of the goal. Since the wing forward must eventually cross the ball or carry it toward the middle of the field to score, the concentrated defenders are in a favorable position to support each other. When defending players are too far apart, support is nonexistent and open space is created for the attacking team.

Containment

Often, inexperienced players will attempt to steal the ball from an opponent by rushing in, hoping the opposition will make an error. This may prove successful with poorly skilled opponents, but at higher levels such play becomes foolhardy. In fact, a skilled forward hopes the defender will rush in and recklessly overcommit. A slight body swerve is all it takes for the forward to slip

by the onrushing defender. The defender must remember never to overcommit or put himself in a position where, if beaten, he cannot quickly recover. He should attempt to contain his opponent, prohibiting the attacker from making a penetrating pass or a dangerous run on goal. Defenders must refrain from taking great risks in trying to steal the ball unless they are positive of success. On defense, it is best to play cautiously and avoid mistakes; gambling and losing may result in a goal for the opposing team. Aggressiveness is a necessary ingredient, but it must be used in a controlled manner. Teams should strive for sound, error-free, defensive soccer. Reckless chances are taken only in desperate circumstances.

Pressuring the Opponent

The game of soccer requires players who can perform the basic skills in a confined area. When tightly marked, attacking players find themselves with a minimum of space and time to control the ball. Tight coverage by defenders is called pressuring. To stymie the opposing attack, the defending team must pressure opponents into misdirected passes and inaccurate shots. Many skillful players perform poorly when their time and space are reduced by defensive pressure.

Depending on coaching preference, some teams will pressure opponents in all parts of the field while others pressure only in their own defensive half, allowing the opposition to freely advance the ball until midfield is reached. Regardless of which method is used, one basic rule must be followed – the closer an opponent moves to the goal, the tighter he must be marked. An opposing forward occupying the critical area in front of the goal must not be given space. A defensive lapse here could prove disastrous. As the opposition moves farther from the goal, it becomes less dangerous and therefore the marking can become less rigorous. The concept of pressuring on defense should be stressed in training sessions so it will carry over into actual game situations.

The Overlap

Defenders who can contribute to the attack are a requirement in modern systems of play. Wing defenders and midfielders should be adept at moving forward and carrying the ball into opposition territory. A common attack method involving these players is called the overlap. As the name suggests, the defender moves forward into an attacking position, overlapping his own teammates. When properly executed, this tactic often catches the opposition by surprise. To be successful, however, the area must first be cleared of opponents. Intelligent diagonal runs by the forwards, designed to draw defenders out of position, will create the open space into which the defender can successfully overlap and launch his attack. Proper timing of the run is essential. If the defender moves forward before the area is cleared, he will lose the element of surprise. To be effective, he must delay his run until the area is open and then sprint forward into the open space.

Defensive Tactics

Great defenders are developed. Superstars are not born to play certain positions. Assuredly, they must be blessed with a certain amount of natural physical ability and must master the basic skills necessary to their craft. However, the game requires much more than physical attributes. Intelligent teamwork is the basis of modern tactical defense. The principles of depth in defense, support, and concentration in defense can only be achieved through players understanding and fulfilling their roles within a group situation. Small-sided games serve a useful purpose in practicing defensive tactics. Virtually all of these principles can be demonstrated in a 3-on-2 or a 4-on-3 practice session. Be sure to concentrate on developing your defensive as well as offensive capabilities. In the modern era of total player involvement, each player must consider himself to be a defender when his team does not have ball possession.

Responsibilities of defending players
- Be goalside of your opponent.
- Do not overcommit.
- Use the sideline and endline as teammates.
- When confronting an opponent who has possession of the ball, use a staggered stance and force the opponent to one side or the other. Do not defend square.
- Do not allow the penetrating pass.
- Maintain communication with your goalkeeper.
- Delay your opponent.
- Be aware of the position of the ball.

Courtesy Tulsa Roughnecks.

6.Attack Tactics

With the onset of sophisticated defensive systems now being used in modern soccer, teams have been forced to develop newer and better methods of attack. Every player must realize his role in the system, for it requires the combined efforts of all players to be successful. Possession of a thunderous shot or clever dribbling ability does not ensure one of being a prolific scorer. Physical attributes must be interwoven with intelligent tactical play. In many instances, a player who does not have the ball may create a scoring opportunity for a teammate by a well-timed run. Where and when to run while not in possession of the ball is a most difficult concept for young players to comprehend. Inexperienced players will benefit by watching professionals move without the ball. All movements are well-calculated and purposeful; energy is not wasted on useless maneuvers. Efficient running to create space, plus the knowledge of where to pass and when to shoot, are basic ingredients of a strong attacking system.

Tactical Aspects of Dribbling

The highly individualistic skill of dribbling, while a vital component of every attack, may often lead to disruption of team play if used in excess. Tactically, it is wise to limit the amount of dribbling in your defensive third of the field, an area where one mistake may result in an opponent's score. Defending players should move the ball quickly and accurately to teammates in more forward positions. Ideally, defending players should concentrate on playing one-touch soccer whenever possible.

In the central portion of the field, usually controlled by the midfielders, dribbling may occur more frequently but still should be used sparingly. Excessive dribbling results in sluggish, predictable midfield play that hinders the entire attack. Quick movement of the ball, primarily one- and two-touch passing, is characteristic of successful, attacking midfield play. The responsibility of the midfield players is important since they dictate the tempo of the attack.

Dribbling can be used to the best advantage in the attacking third of the field. Forwards with the ability to take on a defender and go to the goal are a definite requirement in top-flight soccer. However, excessive dribbling, even in the attacking third of the field, can be a detriment if not used intelligently. The selfish player hurts not only his own performance but also the efforts of his teammates.

Soccer

Creating Space for a Teammate

Although a player may run several miles during a soccer match, the actual time of ball possession is only a few minutes. For the remaining 80-plus minutes, the player finds himself without the ball. Many players think that they can rest during this time if not directly involved in play. Nothing could be further from the truth. Movement without the ball is very important in the overall team effort. Attempting to take defending players into poor defensive positions will contribute to the goal-scoring process just as much as the well-executed pass. Always concentrate on running with a purpose – the purpose of making things easier for your teammates.

Creating Space for Yourself

Everyone who has played the game would agree that it is much easier to execute the necessary skills if given ample time and space in which to operate. However, as a player enters higher levels of play he will find himself tightly marked in most situations. To obtain precious time and sufficient space, each player must find ways to lose the man who is marking him. One of the best methods is change-of-pace running. Avoid running at a constant speed since such movement is predictable and allows the defender to anticipate the intentions of an attacker easily. Be unpredictable in your movements. Jogging, accelerating, and changing directions may cause the defender to hesitate at times, just long enough to allow an attacker open space. Every player must work hard to free himself from the defender marking him and in that way improve his chances of successful play.

Creating space for a teammate. Left wing forward runs diagonally across the middle of the defense, drawing the wing defender toward the center of the field. Space is created in the wing area vacated by the defender.

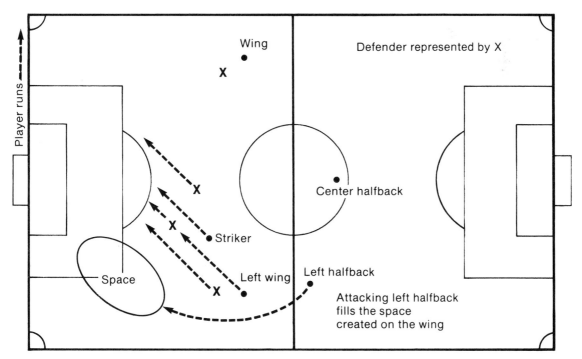

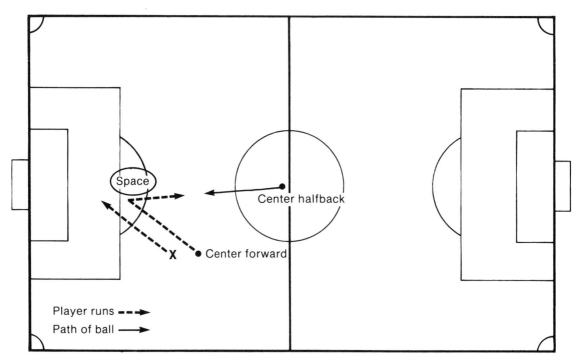

Creating space for yourself. The center forward makes a diagonal run drawing the defender with him. Suddenly, the forward stops and withdraws, creating the desired space in which he can receive and turn with the pass given by his center halfback.

Another method of creating space between yourself and the defender covering you is termed checking off. In order to lose the opponent, you must make a convincing attempt to run past him into a penetrating position, then suddenly stop and withdraw. Such an unexpected change of direction usually increases the distance between yourself and the defender, creating more space and time in which the ball may be controlled and utilized to your best advantage.

Diagonal Running

The direction in which a player makes his runs is very important. Many inexperienced players make a direct run for the opponent's goal as soon as their team has gained possession of the ball. A direct route to goal is not always a good tactic since the defender following will also end up in a central defensive position, a position favorable to the defense. It is much wiser to execute a run that draws the defender away from the goal area. However, some players carry this idea to extremes by consistently directing their runs across the field when trying to get open for a pass, neglecting to penetrate the opposing defense. It is very easy to defend such a run that merely moves in front of the defense.

The best type of run is directed diagonally through the defense. Such runs draw defenders away from their central positions and penetrate dangerous attacking areas. Diagonal runs also create space in front of the attacker where he can receive a pass from a teammate. The penetrating nature of the diagonal run can cause confusion in the defense and lead to mistakes. The attacking players should capitalize on these defensive errors. All players not in possession of the ball should strive to use intelligent running that will create problems for the defense while at the same time gain a better position for themselves.

Diagonal running. Diagonal penetrating run by #10 draws the defender away from the central position and creates space for #9 in a dangerous scoring area. The winger, #8, takes his man away from the play. Diagonal runs serve two purposes: to penetrate the defense and also to draw defenders away from the goal area.

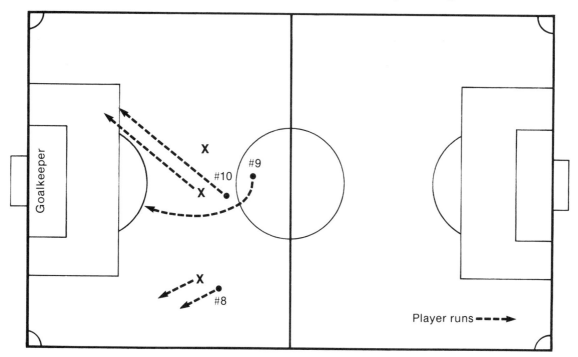

Soccer

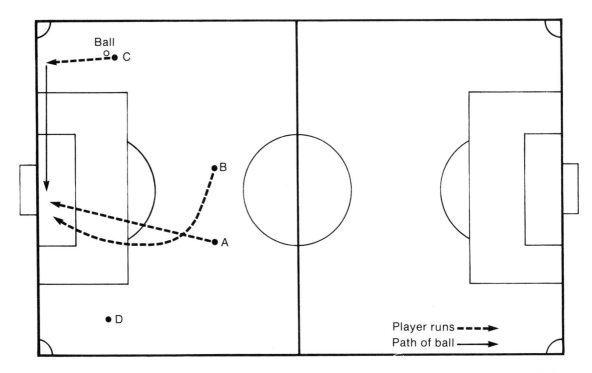

Tactical running patterns. Player C with the ball serves across to the near post. Striker B bends a run to the far post while striker A sprints to the near post. Timing of the runs is very important; the strikers must not arrive in the penalty area too early or they will be marked by opponents. Just as the ball is about to be served, the strikers should be sprinting into the penalty area.

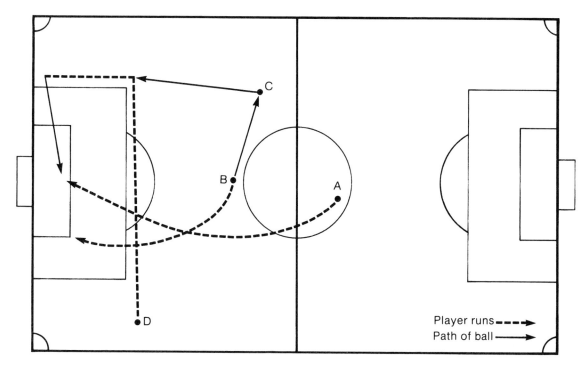

Player runs ‑ ‑ ‑ ►
Path of ball ———►

Tactical running patterns. Server A plays the ball to target B who passes to support player C. C passes the ball into the open space on the wing area. Player D makes a cross-field run and collects the ball, dribbles to the endline, and crosses the ball to the near post. Player B has made a run to the far post while the original server A has run to the near post.

Soccer

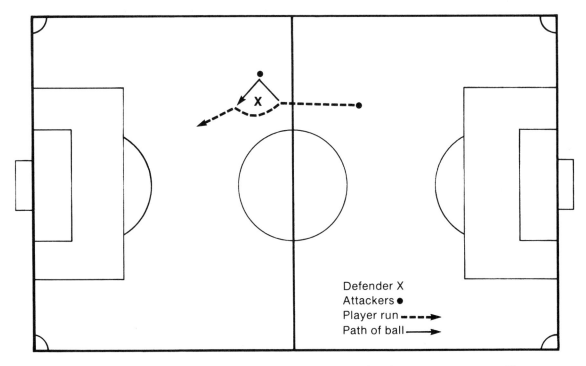

Defender X
Attackers ●
Player run ▪▪▪▪▶
Path of ball ──▶

Running with the ball; the give and go pass. When dribbling the ball, go directly at your opponent until he commits to you. At that moment, pass to your teammate and sprint to open space for a return pass.

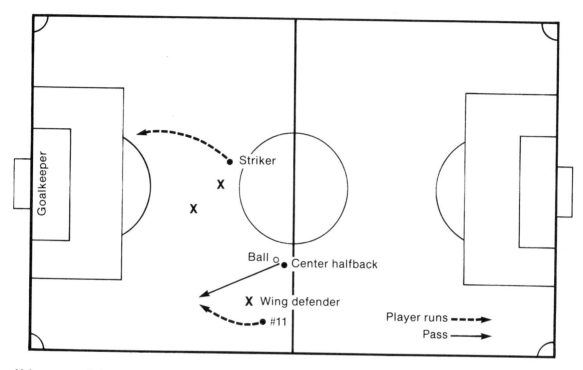

Utilizing space behind the defense. A penetrating pass directed into space behind the wing defender X frees the wing forward #11 for a strike at goal. Proper timing of the pass and run is crucial for success.

Running While in Possession of the Ball

When a player has possession of the ball, the running tactics will change. When dribbling, it is best to run directly at the opponent, forcing the defending player to commit himself one way or another. If the defender decides to tackle, the attacker should pass the ball to a teammate in a more dangerous scoring position. A well-timed pass will leave the defender out of position once he has overcommitted himself. If the defender elects not to confront the attacker but retreats to contain him, the attacking player should then dribble toward the goal and attempt the shot. In any event, running directly at the defender while dribbling will force him to make a decision and create possible scoring options for the attack.

Utilize Space Behind the Defense

Many defending players are only conscious of what is in front of them. This fault is sometimes referred to as ball watching and is a common mistake among inexperienced players. The attacking team can take advantage of a ball-watching defender by playing the ball into open space behind the defense. A well-timed run coupled with an accurate pass may free a teammate for an attempt on goal. Attackers must take care not to locate themselves in an offside position when receiving the pass. If proper timing of the pass and run is achieved, use of space behind the defense is one of the best methods for causing disorganization among the opposition.

Shooting Tactics

One major fault in many teams is failure to shoot when presented with the opportunity. Chances to shoot on goal must not be wasted, especially at higher levels of play where improved defensive systems limit scoring opportunities. The best shot is one that the goalkeeper doesn't expect. Many goals are scored on shots that are not well struck but that catch the goalkeeper flatfooted. Forwards must learn to release their shot quickly in all sorts of positions. Midfielders, playing a vital role in the attack, can attempt shots from outside the penalty area. Long-range shooting will sometimes draw the defense out from their goal in an effort to block shots and consequently create openings for attackers in forward areas. All players must acquire the ability to move equally well to left or right and to shoot with either foot. Such ability is a prime requisite if a player expects to score with regularity.

The angle at which the shot is taken is very critical to the success or failure of any attack. Shots driven on goal from the wing areas have a poor chance of finding the back of the net since the shooting angle has been reduced. Most goals are scored from more central positions

A member of the Detroit Express gives his all to the play. *Courtesy Detroit Express. Photo by Ron Winter.*

Oscar Fabbiani, 1979 league scoring title holder, dribbles around a defender to score a goal for Tampa Bay. *Courtesy Tampa Bay Rowdies. Photo by Richard S. Spann.*

Graham Pay of the Portland Timbers tackles an opponent to steal the ball. *Courtesy Portland Timbers. Photo by Bil Hunt.*

A member of the Detroit Express leaps to head the ball. *Courtesy Detroit Express. Photo by Larry F. Winter.*

The Detroit Express blocks a pass to an opposing player. *Courtesy Detroit Express. Photo by Larry F. Winter.*

A Houston Hurricane tackles an opponent to control the ball. *Courtesy Houston Hurricane. Photo by William LoDato.*

The Houston Hurricane battles an opponent for possession of the ball. *Courtesy Houston Hurricane. Photo by George L. Craig II.*

where a wide angle to goal is provided. For the greatest chance of success, a team must create numerous scoring opportunities in the most dangerous scoring zones.

Corner Kicks

Corner kicks provide an excellent opportunity for goal scoring. Most teams have designed special set-plays for use on corner kicks with the primary purpose of freeing an attacking player for an attempt on goal. Those teams blessed with a tall, strong header will usually try to loft the corner kick into an area where the attacker can head in a score.

It is very important that the corner kick can be centered 8–10 yards in front of the goal. A ball placed in that area may make the goalkeeper hesitate, while deciding whether or not to leave the goal area. The slight indecision can result in a mistake and a goal. Many variations of corner kick plays have been developed by inventive coaches and players in attempts to confuse

Shooting tactics. Attacking teams should attempt to create numerous scoring opportunities in the most dangerous scoring zone centrally located in front of the goal.

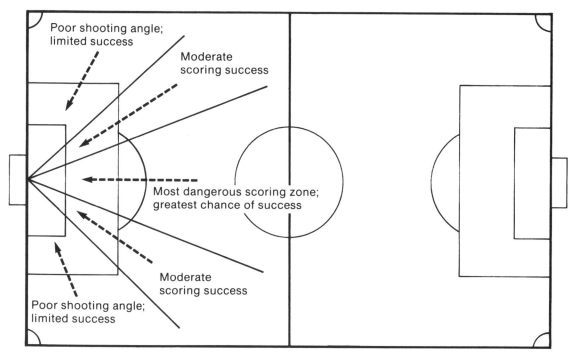

Soccer

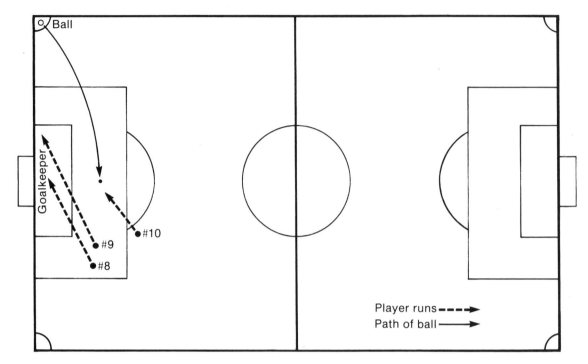

Corner kick. Timed runs are made by three attacking players, #8, #9, and #10. Players #8 and #9 run to create space in front of the goal for #10 to fill. Player #10 must delay his run until space has been vacated by #8 and #9.

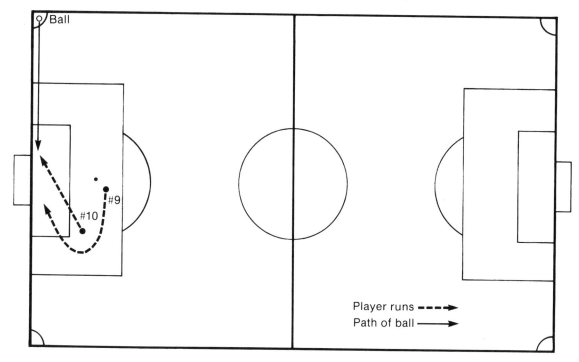

Near post corner kick play. The ball is driven powerfully to the near post where #10 runs to meet and deflect the ball into the goal. Player #9 curls his run to the far post in case the ball sails to that area.

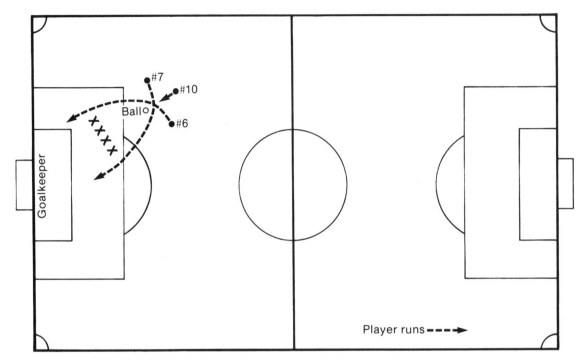

Direct free kick. Player #6 runs over the ball to the right of the defensive wall, player #7 follows with a run to the left, player #10 then follows with a strike at goal.

defenders and create goals. In recent years the near-post corner kick has gained popularity at the professional level. Rather than lofting the ball into the goal area, the kick is driven hard to the near post where a forward has timed his run to meet the ball and deflect it on goal. The sudden change of direction in the flight of the ball often fools the goalkeeper.

Regardless of which type of set-play a team decides to use, a sufficient portion of practice time must be devoted to perfecting corner kick plays. If not, many excellent scoring chances will be wasted.

Throw-ins and Free Kicks

Throw-ins are another aspect of the game that often are forgotten in training sessions. Every team should have a variety of throw-in plays, especially when the ball is being put into play near the opponent's goal area. This is not to say that the plans cannot be altered; often the game will dictate that a change must be made. However, every player should understand the importance of throw-ins and their function in the attack.

In modern soccer, more and more goals are being scored from dead-ball situations (i.e., free kicks, throw-ins, corner kicks, penalty kicks). During the 1974 World Cup final between West Germany and Holland, two of the three goals scored were from dead-ball situations. A great emphasis must be placed on perfecting the restart plays, including both direct and indirect free kicks. Players who have the ability to bend or curve their free kicks are especially valuable to a team. The lethal left foot of Brazilian international Rivelino has scored many goals from curving free kicks. He mastered the technique of bending his drives around the defensive wall and into the goal. Needless to say, most teams do not have an individual who can score in such fashion. Well-conceived plays involving two or three players can be just as effective, however, if properly applied.

Responsibilities of attacking players
- Build the attack.
- Maintain ball possession.
- Look for the penetrating (killer) pass.
- Create space for teammates.
- Creative dribbling in the attacking third of the field.
- Interchange of positions (mobility).
- Make yourself available for passes from teammates.
- Capitalize on scoring opportunities.

Soccer

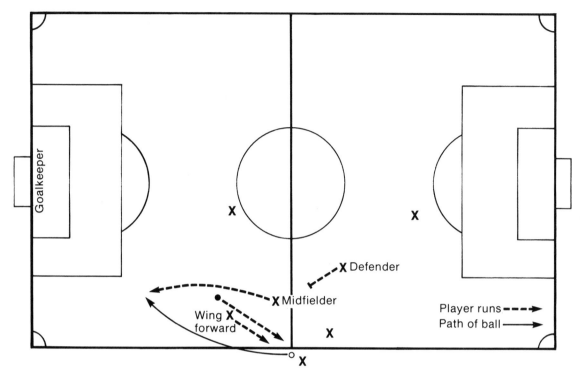

Throw-in. The wing forward, who is tightly marked, runs toward the thrower. The midfielder runs into the space vacated by the wing forward to receive the throw-in.

7. Systems of Play

Just as living organisms have evolved or changed over great periods of the earth's history, soccer has also undergone changes throughout its existence. Teams and coaches have constantly striven to perfect the ultimate system of play to ensure victory. The debate about which system is best still echoes through most soccer circles and is evidenced by the changing philosophies over the years. However, the perfect system of play does not exist; it is a misconception to believe that systems win games. Players who have been molded by proper coaching into a smooth, functioning whole win games. Many ingredients, ranging from proper fitness and technique to specific match preparation, comprise the successful team. The system or organization of players on the field is only one factor among many that contribute to either success or failure.

The organization of players on the field is similar regardless of the system or formation used. Basic principles must be applied: depth in attack and defense, support play by teammates, and a high degree of skill coupled with intelligent tactical play. Whether your team uses the old WM system or the modern 4-3-3, once play starts the results depend upon how well the players apply the basics of the game. A common mistake made by many coaches is choosing a system first, then placing the players into that formational setup. The system must be designed to suit the players; the capabilities of a team's personnel must be the deciding factors in dictating the correct system for that specific group. Every team should therefore discover which system will best suit its needs and limitations.

Since a variety of systems have been implemented over the years, a discussion of a few of the more popular ones will give some guidelines to the changes that have occurred as the modern game evolved. When describing a system such as the 4-3-3, the first number refers to defensive players, the second to midfield players, and the third to attacking players. The numbering includes only the 10 field players, not the goalkeeper.

2-3-5 System

In the early 1900s, most teams assembled their players on the field in a formation suited for those who enjoy attacking soccer. The prevalent system was the 2-3-5, where 5 attacking players were supported by 3 midfielders, 2 fullbacks and, of course, the goalkeeper. The center halfback was the key figure and had to fill dual roles, both in attack and defense. The 2 fullbacks were positioned in a zonal defense marking the areas usually occupied by the opposing inside forwards.

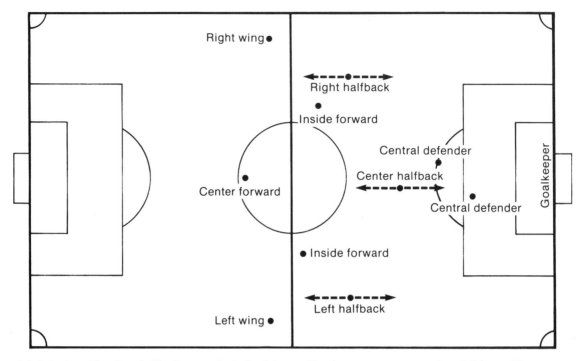

2-3-5 System. The three halfbacks carry the bulk of the workload, supporting on attack and defense. The wing halfbacks function in the same role as wing defenders in the more recent 4-3-3.

They played in tandem with one diagonally behind the other to create depth in defense. The right and left halfbacks marked the opponent's wingers, while the center halfback marked the center forward.

Such a formation made the job of the midfielders difficult since they were expected to be an integral part of attack while also being responsible for marking the opposing forwards. The 5 attacking players were usually positioned with a center forward, 2 conventional wingers, and 2 inside forwards. Their principal job was to attack, and they did not get involved extensively in the defensive scheme of the team. The system had obvious limitations, since players were restricted in their roles, and it certainly did not agree with the modern version of total football in which all players must have attacking and defensive responsibilities.

The basic positioning of the players has been modified in this system. Some teams chose to withdraw one of their inside forwards who would assume a trailing position behind the front runners, aiding the midfielders in the central area of the field. In general, however, the player mobility was limited and play was predictable.

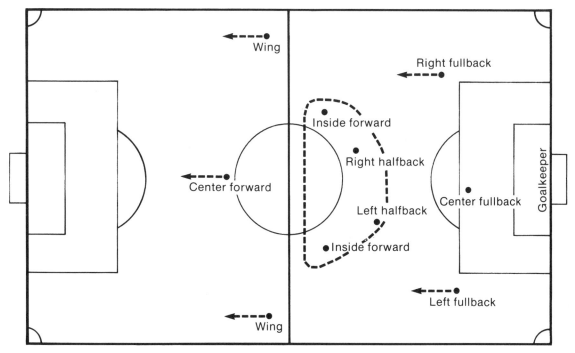

3-2-5 System. The inside forward and halfbacks do the bulk of the running, controlling the midfield areas. With only one central defender, the system is vulnerable at the back.

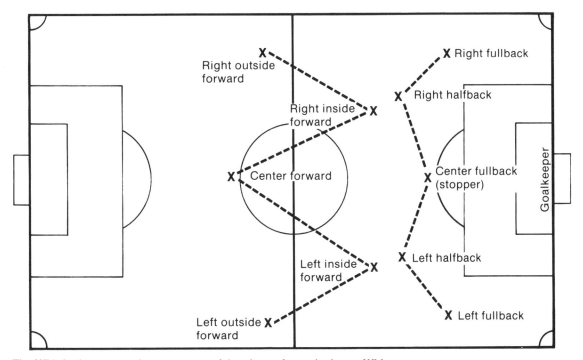

The WM. In this system, the positioning of the players forms the letters WM.

Soccer

WM System (3-2-5)

As coaches attempted to improve on the 2-3-5 formation, Herbert Chapman of FC Arsenal devised a variation of the system. The new formation, known as the WM, was constructed upon the premise of midfield buildup with the additional help of the inside forwards who were to withdraw to midfield positions and become playmakers as well as goalscorers. The center forward remained upfront to spearhead the attack as did the right and left wingers. The positioning of the 5 attackers resembled the letter W with 3 front runners and 2 withdrawn forwards. The wingers were very important in creating scoring opportunities; they had to be adept at dribbling and taking on opponents. Two halfbacks were positioned in the central zone of the field with the responsibility of marking the opposing inside forwards. They were aided in control of midfield by there own inside forwards. The 3 back defenders in the WM were arranged so the wing defenders marked the opposing wingers and the center fullback marked the center forward.

The WM system had many disadvantages. The strict man-to-man marking of the 3 back defenders left the defense particularly vulnerable to intelligent running by opponents; runs aimed to draw defenders out of position created scoring opportunities for the opposition. Also, only one center fullback was employed; the sweeper of today was nonexistent. Since the center fullback was given man-to-man responsibility, the system lacked adequate support cover for the defenders.

4-2-4 System

During the World Cup matches of 1958, a new, innovative system gained widespread popularity when Brazil used a 4-2-4 setup to become champions of the soccer world. Blessed with great players such as Pelé, Didi, and Garrincha, Brazilian coach Vincente Feola implemented a formation that had 4 back defenders, 2 midfielders or linkmen, and 4 attacking forwards. The linkmen, who operated in the midfield position, were given an important although difficult assignment. When their team was in possession of the ball and on attack, the linkmen functioned as extra forwards supporting the front runners. On defense, they became extra defenders in the central portion of the field.

The back 4 were comprised of 2 central defenders and a right and left back. The wing defenders in the 4-2-4 were given a bit more freedom than their predecessors, and the overlap added yet another dimension to the attack. The front players, consisting of 2 wingers and 2 inside forwards, were assigned to finish the onslaughts on goal. They were not rigidly fixed in position but displayed a great deal of movement both with or without the ball. At times, one of the wingers would assume a withdrawn position in order to receive passes from the defense and also to aid the linkmen in control of midfield.

The 4-2-4 system exemplified the changing philosophies and concepts of play. Player mobility was given more emphasis and great importance. Each player was required to understand and accept the responsibilities of a teammate should position switching occur. There were still improvements to be made and better methods of play to evolve, but the 4-2-4 introduced a new, creative era in soccer.

4-2-4 System. Player mobility is emphasized in this system. The two midfielders function as a link between the attack and the defense.

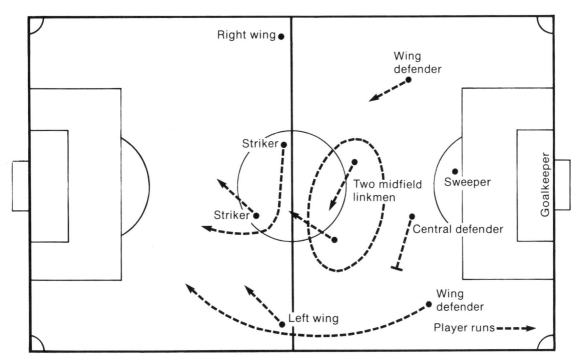

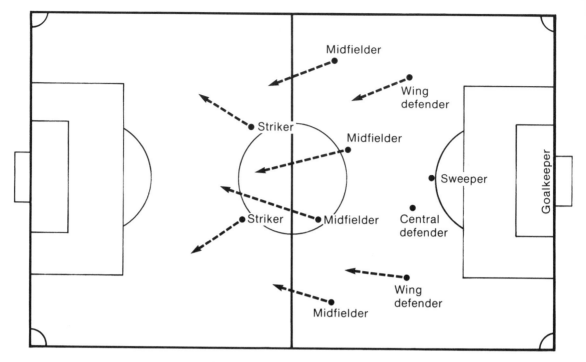

4-4-2 System. Four players are positioned in the midfield area. On attack, the midfielders must assume more forward positions in space created by the front strikers. Wing defenders also move forward in support of the midfield.

4-4-2 System

Control of the midfield is vital to the success of every team. Attacking movements are often initiated in this area, as well as attempts to thwart the efforts of opponents to build their attack. As a consequence, certain teams have chosen to position 4 players in the midfield zone, in an attempt to provide maximum control in that area. The midfielders are supported from behind by 4 back defenders, while 2 forwards are positioned as dual strikers in the attacking zone. At first glance the 4-4-2 might seem like a defense-oriented system, although theoretically it is not. True, the fullbacks and midfielders provide overwhelming numbers for defense when the need arises, but when moving to the offensive the midfielders and defenders move forward to assume attacking roles and the 4-4-2 actually becomes very similar to the 4-2-4 system. If the midfielders do not exhibit attacking support, the 4-4-2 does indeed become defense oriented, relying on only two strikers to create goals. Such strategy is not conducive to consistent scoring and is not in accord with the modern philosophy of the game.

Catenaccio

Fans and players alike enjoy an attacking, wide-open style of soccer. Such tactics, although pleasing to the eye, are not always in the best interests of the team since the tactics become vulnerable to swift counterattack. At the highest levels of play where winning is a must, certain coaches have adopted a very conservative approach to the game. A system built upon those guidelines appeared in Italy several years ago, based on the principle "If the other team doesn't score, the worst possible result for our team will be a draw." Called catenaccio and designed to provide an almost impenetrable defense, the players were organized as 5 back defenders, 3–4 midfielders, and 1–2 forwards (depending on the coach's personal preference). The tactics were successful in accomplishing that aim – fewer goals. However, such a style made for a slow, unimaginative type of soccer. Most spectators objected, and many players concurred with the fans. Today catenaccio has almost disappeared, a victim of its inability to evolve with the modern game.

Catenaccio System. A defensive-oriented formation, the catenaccio system concentrates many players in the dangerous scoring zones. One or two strikers are positioned in forward positions to generate the attack.

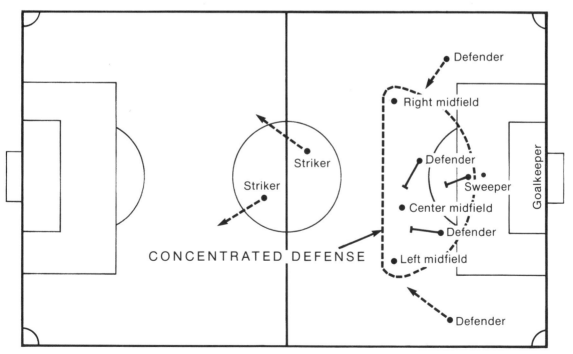

4-3-3 System

The ever-continuing search for the ideal system has led soccer enthusiasts to yet another variation similar to the 4-2-4 of Brazil. In an effort to devise a formation that requires all-around players who are in constant motion, the 4-3-3 system has generally replaced the 4-2-4. As the numbering of the system indicates, there are 4 defenders, 3 midfielders, and 3 attackers. The 4-3-3 requires players to have both attacking and defensive capabilities, since interchanging positions is vital if the system is played correctly. Eleven players attack; eleven defend. Even the goalkeeper is expected to contribute to the attack.

The 4 back defenders and 3 midfielders provide adequate numbers to cover critical space in the defensive third of the field. Usually, one of the central defenders assumes the role of sweeper. He is the free man in the defense and is not given man-to-man marking responsibilities. The other central defender is called the stopper. He is assigned tight man-to-man marking of the opponent's center forward. The right and left wing defenders cover the opposing wingers. With 3 midfielders, the 4-3-3 allows more freedom of movement among the halfbacks than was the case in the 4-2-4 system. The midfielders, besides aiding in the defense, must also support their forwards from behind; otherwise, the strikers will find themselves outnumbered in the opponent's defensive third of the field.

At the professional level, most forwards are very tightly marked, and midfielders have undertaken more of a goal-scoring role. Intelligent movements by the strikers are expected to create space, allowing midfielders to move forward for attempts on goal. Overlapping runs by the defenders also add extra men into the attack. The emphasis on mobility in the 4-3-3 permits concentration of players for attack and defense, a tactic not possible in earlier systems.

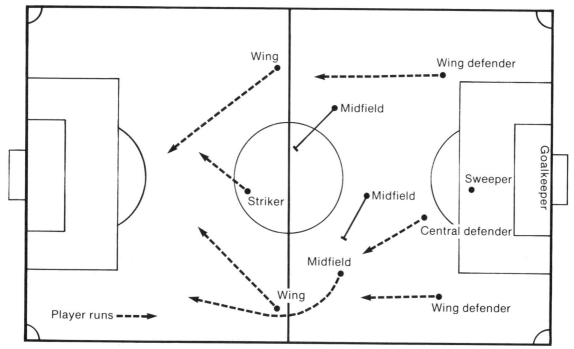

4-3-3 System. Total soccer is the theme of the 4-3-3 system. All players must possess attacking and defending abilities with midfielders and even defenders moving forward to score goals.

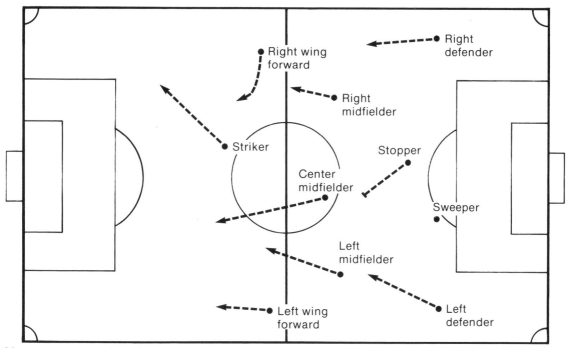

Movement patterns of the 4-3-3 system. The center striker makes a run to the wing area, creating space for the center midfielder to move forward into an attacking position.

111

Courtesy Tulsa Roughnecks.

8. Fitness

Players will usually run a distance of approximately 4-6 miles in a 90-minute match. At such a work rate, total fitness is an absolute requirement. All techniques and skills previously covered in this book are useless if the performer is not in top physical condition. Fatigue due to poor fitness diminishes skill performance, results in loss of quickness, and frequently leads to mental errors as the player becomes exhausted in the latter stages of a game. Knowing that a player cannot rely on natural ability alone, serious students of soccer work hard to maintain peak physical condition. Fitness, coupled with a high level of skill, must be achieved if a player is to be successful against tough competition.

Since a player is required to encounter an assortment of physical activities during play, his training must vary accordingly. The ideal training schedule should prepare a team for actual match conditions, encompassing the entire gamut of sprints, twists, and turns. Methods of training vary from team to team, depending on the strengths and weaknesses of individual players. A variety of training methods may be used and incorporated into the overall fitness program designed to achieve match fitness.

Warm-up

Prior to any strenuous training session, each player should undergo a warm-up period. Warm-up activities increase blood and muscle temperatures that prepare the body for physical exertion. The session may consist of a variety of exercises including jogging, ball juggling, ball gymnastics, and running games such as relay races, tag, etc. Flexibility exercises are also an integral part of every warm-up. Stretching the various muscle groups helps improve player agility as well as prevent unnecessary muscle injuries.

Two general types of warm-up can be used in preparation for training. An unrelated warm-up consists of exercises that increase body temperature but do not involve actual soccer skills, such as jumping jacks, pull ups, and running in place. It is better to warm-up with exercises related to soccer skills such as dribbling, passing, and ball juggling. A related warm-up serves two purposes: it achieves the desired physiological effects (increased body temperature) and provides skill practice.

Duration of the warm-up period varies, depending upon individual team members. The session should be long enough and intense enough to cause the players to perspire – usually 15 to 20 minutes.

Soccer

Courtesy California Surf. MVP Sports Photography.

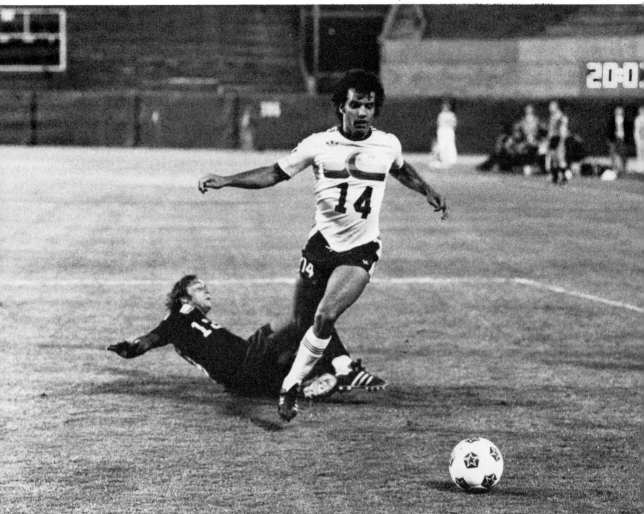

Warm-up Exercises

Individual

- Place the ball at your feet. Run in place, touching the top of the ball with the sole of the foot on each step, alternating feet (30-40 seconds at maximum speed).
- Place the ball at your feet. Stand beside the ball and, keeping the feet together, jump over the ball and back at maximum speed (30-40 seconds).

- Push-ups on the ball.
- One-touch tapping of the ball between the insides of the feet (30 – 40 seconds at maximum speed).
- Ball juggling, using the feet, thighs, and head.

With a partner

- Sit-up position for one player, other standing. As one player sits up, his partner lobs a ball to him and he must return it by heading. Repeat 25 times, then switch positions.
- Stand back-to-back with a partner. Spread the legs and bend forward at the waist; handing the ball through the legs to your partner. Straighten up and receive the ball over your head from your partner. Repeat 30 times.
- Both partners assume a push-up position facing each other, about 2 feet apart. A ball is placed on the ground between the players. Push the ball back and forth, using the head, as rapidly as possible while remaining in a push-up position (30-second duration).
- Ball juggling with a partner. Two-touch, then one-touch interpassing without allowing the ball to hit the ground.

Soccer

Group warm-up
- 5 players vs. 2 players – possession game in restricted space. Emphasize player movement, interchanging of positions.
- Mass dribbling. Each player, with a ball, dribbles in a designated area while avoiding other players in that area. Emphasize movement, ball control, and field vision.
- Interpassing among 3 or more players while moving around the field.

Flexibility Training

Flexibility exercises that increase an individual's range of motion are an important part of the overall soccer fitness program. Player agility is a requirement for performing most soccer skills. The most recent and beneficial method of ensuring maximum flexibility is static stretching. As the term implies, a player stretches as far as possible and holds (static) that position for 15–30 seconds. *Do not* bounce; bouncing increases the chances of accidentally pulling or even tearing muscles. Merely stretch to your maximum, without great pain, and hold that position. It is very important that flexibility exercises do not become competitions between team members; each individual knows his abilities and should stretch accordingly. Don't overdo it – strained muscles may result through extending beyond your physical limits.

Running

In order to develop the endurance required to play 90 minutes of nonstop action, most training programs include types of running similar to that experienced in the game. Distance running at a relatively constant pace helps develop general endurance and stamina, but soccer entails much more than distance running. It must be complemented by other forms that prepare players for sprinting runs that occur in a match. Europeans have devised a running program called fartlek that consists of cross-country running at varying speeds, up and down hills as well as on level surfaces, constantly changing speeds. The entire team runs long distances simulating the style of running that will occur under actual game conditions. If the running surface permits, players will benefit by dribbling a ball as they train.

Weight Training

Weight training, if properly supervised, can be a valuable addition to the fitness program. All players need some form of strength training to prepare them for the physical demands of the game. The belief that a player will become muscle-bound and lose agility through the use of

weights is a fallacy. Flexibility exercises will maintain a player's agility even as the individual increases in strength. Development of upper body strength is necessary for the player to withstand the bumps and bruises that inevitably occur when challenging for the ball. Weight training for the legs may also be helpful, although the great amount of running and kicking in team practice is usually adequate for developing sufficient strength and endurance.

Interval Training

Interval training consists of periods of intense physical activity (work) followed by a short recovery period (rest). The interval method has gained great popularity in recent years because it closely resembles the physical stress encountered in a game. Under match conditions, players often endure periods of intense action, such as sprinting runs with the ball, while catching their breath whenever they can find a spare moment. Many of the modern training methods such as pressure training, functional training, and circuit training are considered forms of interval training.

The work intervals of intense physical activity should last 30-90 seconds and should be followed by a rest period of 60-180 seconds. The length of the rest period depends on the amount of strenuous activity and the individuals involved. The recovery period is immediately followed by another work interval, then rest. This cycle should be repeated as many times as the coach feels necessary.

The intensity of the interval training program can be changed by adjusting variables in the work schedule. These variables include rate of work during the exercise period, length of the rest interval, and the number of repetitions of the work interval.

Functional Training

Functional training incorporates actual game situations into the exercise session, stressing the technical or tactical aspects of a specific playing position. For example, a functional drill might have 3 or 4 players practicing an overlap by a wing defender, each making the designated run just as in actual game conditions. Functional drills are repeated again and again until the coach feels his players have mastered the concept. As players become more adept, it is imperative that functional training proceed at top speed to simulate match play. Fitness, as well as technical and tactical improvement, will result from the same drills.

Pressure Training

Pressure training in practice sessions is another excellent method of combining skill training with physical fitness. The pressure is applied by requiring a player to repeat a skill at maximum speed within a specified period. A possible drill might be a player jumping and heading away several rapidly served balls for 1 minute. Rest 30 seconds before repeating the exercise. An alternative drill designed to improve shooting skills uses 10-15 balls. The coach rolls one after another to different sections of the penalty area and requires a forward to chase and then strike each ball on goal, concluding the drill when all of the balls have been shot. Pressure training forces a player to perform skills under fatigued conditions against the clock. Such a situation closely simulates actual game conditions in which players are subjected to intense pressure from opponents while in a state of physical stress.

Circuit Training

Constructing a training circuit consisting of different stations located at various parts of the field allows the coach to cover a number of objectives in a relatively short time. Each station is designed for a specific purpose (fitness, skill training, etc.) and can be completed within a specified time.

Players, usually working in pairs, move from station to station until the entire circuit has been completed. Each player will work at maximum intensity for 1 minute at each station, rest while his partner works for 1 minute, and then both are allotted 1 minute to walk to the next station. Work and rest intervals may vary, but a common standard is approximately 1-1½ minutes of high-intensity work followed by 2-3 minutes of rest. Since each station will take approximately 3 minutes to complete, an entire 15-station circuit can be completed in less than 1 hour.

There are many types of stations that can be included in the training circuit. Examples would be weight training, skipping rope, abdominal strengthening exercises, obstacle course, and work with a medicine ball. Actual game skills such as heading, dribbling, or shooting can easily be incorporated into the circuit. Coaches should plan their training circuit according to their particular player situation, concentrating on improving player weaknesses. The circuit method need not be used every day but as a change of pace from the normal practice routine.

Sample abdominal exercises used in the circuit
- Sit-ups (normal).
- Partners sit, facing one another, and interlock feet. Do sit-ups in unison at maximum speed.
- Leg raises. Lying flat on the ground, raise the legs 6 inches off the ground and hold for 10-15 seconds. Repeat several times.

Soccer

- Heading sit-ups. As one partner does sit-ups, the other serves a ball that is headed back to him.
- One player lies on the ground and holds the ankles of his partner who is standing behind him. The player on the ground lifts his legs up to a vertical position and then drops them to the ground. Repeat 20 times.
- Rowing sit-ups. Lie on the ground with legs raised 12 inches. With a rowing motion, bring the knees to the chest, then extend. Repeat.

Games for Fitness

As many players will openly admit, fitness training can often become tedious and boring for those involved. It is refreshing to sometimes use fun games in the training sessions to generate enthusiasm and relieve the monotony of everyday practice. A variety of games will make practice enjoyable and also serve to achieve the desired fitness level.

Leapfrog Races

Almost everyone has played leapfrog during their childhood, but few realize the conditioning benefits of the game. While leaping over other teammates, each player is developing upper body (chest and arms) as well as leg muscle strength. Divide the team into two groups and leapfrog race over a distance of 50-60 yards. Most players will be exhausted.

Soccer Tag

The center circle is a good area in which to play soccer tag. The team, divided into two equal squads, lines up around the perimeter of the circle. Members of each squad are numbered, and one squad is initially designated as the "it" team. When the coach shouts out a player's number, that player enters the circle and attempts to tag his identical number on the opposing team who has also entered the circle. When "it" has tagged his opponent, the situation is reversed. Players must continue the game for 1–2 minutes and then are replaced by two fresh players.

Relay Races

Relay races are one method of including sprint training in a fun game situation. The type of relay may vary; a relay without the ball, a race requiring dribbling the ball through a maze of objects, or a relay in which each player must carry a teammate on his back while dribbling. As an added incentive, the winning team should be rewarded.

Fox-Hunter Game

In a restricted area, players dribble a ball while changing speeds and direction. On a signal from the coach, several players without a ball enter the area and attempt to kick any ball they can out of the area. The objective is for the foxes (players dribbling) to elude the hunters (players without a ball) for as long as possible. The fox who maintains ball possession for the longest time is the winner.

Small-Side Soccer Games

Utilizing a reduced number of players for each team, small-side soccer games are one of the best methods of achieving total physical effort for a limited period. A small field is marked off, usually about 50 yards long and 30 yards wide. Two teams, consisting of 2–4 players each, are matched against one another for periods of 4–5 minutes of total, all-out effort. Mini-tournaments can be organized with the winning team receiving a prize. These games will aid in developing skills commonly used in actual game situations and in addition will provide still another variation of fitness training.

Year-Round Fitness Program

It is imperative that soccer players maintain an adequate level of fitness throughout the year, even during the off-season. The easiest and most enjoyable method is to play soccer all year, but if that is not possible, alternative types of exercises must be substituted.

Soccer

When planning a year-long training program for the athlete, consider three periods of time: off-season, pre-season, and in-season. Off-season conditioning should concentrate on developing general endurance capacity, otherwise known as cardiovascular fitness. This can be accomplished through continuous forms of exercise such as long-distance running and fartlek. Off-season weight-training is also beneficial for improving strength and endurance.

Pre-season training (6–8 weeks before the actual season) should include more match-related fitness drills to aid in preparation for actual game competition. Sessions should include training for quick starts and stops, change-of-pace running, explosive acceleration, and extensive work with the ball. Rather than concentrate entirely on general endurance capacity, pre-season training should enhance local muscle endurance.

In-season training maintains the optimal fitness level needed for game competition. Functional training comprises a large portion of the in-season sessions, combining both technical and tactical exercises to sharpen basic skills such as passing and shooting. Less time should be devoted to pure fitness training since players, by that time, should be physically fit.

Regardless of whether a player is training during an off-, pre-, or in-season period, it is very important that a ball be included in the sessions whenever possible. Along with physical fitness, development of excellent ball skills is of utmost importance.

9. Indoor Soccer

A new version of soccer has emerged upon the American sports scene and is gaining great popularity as a spectator sport. Indoor soccer, being played at the high school, college, and professional levels, provides fast, exciting action for players and fans alike. Five field players plus a goalkeeper comprise a typical indoor team. Due to the reduced area of the playing surface and the bank shots off the perimeter walls, high-scoring games are the rule rather than the exception, with the goalkeepers assuming a very important role in the indoor game. Nonstop action interspersed with frequent goals – two characteristics that are endearing to the American sports fan – epitomize indoor soccer.

In many respects, indoor and outdoor soccer are quite similar. Although indoor soccer is unique, the transition from one to the other is not especially difficult for most players. However, the few significant indoor rule changes have created major differences in tactical play.

Lack of the offside rule. The traditional offside rule has been waived indoors, creating a wide-open attacking style of play. Defenders must constantly be aware of opposing forwards positioning themselves in areas behind the defense, a perfectly legal tactic indoors. Limited field space coupled with lack of the offside rule are major factors leading to the high amount of goal scoring indoors.

Playing the ball off perimeter walls. Most indoor soccer fields are enclosed by some type of perimeter wall, whether it be a high school gymnasium or the hockey rinks where professional indoor soccer is played. These walls are considered part of the field of play, allowing players to direct the ball off the side and back boundaries. The walls serve as extra players, providing an excellent surface for give-and-go passing, while allowing nonstop play since the ball rarely leaves the field area. Shots rebounding off the back walls at varying angles make the goalkeeper's job quite strenuous and even hazardous at times. Intelligent tactical use of the perimeter wall serves as a great advantage.

Unlimited substitution. An additional rule difference between indoor soccer and the traditional outdoor game concerns the player substitution law. International rules impose strict, limited substitution of players outdoors, allowing only two substituted per team in a match. In addition, once a player is substituted for or ejected from a game, he is not permitted to return. As a result, limited substitution forces players to pace themselves over the 90-minute match since it would be impossible to perform at maximum effort for the entire duration.

Soccer

Indoor soccer, designed to be played at a very fast pace, has waived the traditional rule and allows unlimited substitution of players. Free substitution permits the players to perform at their maximum work rate for short periods before getting a rest. Constant line changes, much on the same order as professional hockey, replace the exhausted players with fresh players and allow for the accelerated pace characteristic of indoor soccer.

124

Indoor Soccer

Soccer purists will argue that the indoor game, due to its similarity to ice hockey, really isn't soccer at all. However, the fundamentals of both indoor and outdoor soccer are the same. Players must demonstrate the basic skills of passing, dribbling, shooting, and receiving balls in a restricted area under pressure of opponents. Indoor soccer even presents certain advantages; for instance, it provides playing time when adverse weather conditions make outdoor fields unplayable, allowing for year-round participation in the sport. Also, the high degree of technique (skill) development necessary for play in the limited space indoors will carry over into the outdoor game. The concept of total soccer is an integral part of the indoor game, requiring all players to develop both attacking and defending capabilities.

Major Indoor Soccer League

The formation of the Major Indoor Soccer League (MISL) has elevated indoor soccer to the professional level in the United States. During the inaugural 1978-1979 season, six cities fielded teams with expansion a reality. Playing in major sporting arenas throughout the country, indoor soccer has already attracted sell-out crowds in Philadelphia and St. Louis and is realizing quick success as a spectator sport.

Professional indoor soccer will aid in the overall development of the American player, providing high-level competition and playing experience. The MISL has placed restrictions on the number of foreign players (noncitizens) allowed each team. As a result, quality American players are getting an opportunity to demonstrate their abilities at the professional level. The game is played on artificial turf that is laid down over a wood or an ice base. The lack of space forces players to improve their skills and their ability to play the ball quickly. Development of mental quickness is necessary since tight conditions require players to make lightning-quick decisions. Quickness of foot, body, and mind are qualities that must be developed if American teams are to be successful at the international level. Indoor soccer provides valuable training under game conditions that will help to attain these important attributes.

The MISL Rules of Play

Field. Dimensions are smaller than a regulation outdoor field. The length is approximately 200 feet and the width 85 feet. The playing surface is surrounded by a perimeter wall. The player benches are located at midfield, behind the wall.

Ball. Regulation in size and weight, the ball is 27-28 inches in circumference and weighs 14-16 ounces.

Goal. Smaller in size than a regulation outdoor goal, it stands 6 feet 6 inches high and is 12 feet wide. It is placed into the boards.

Soccer

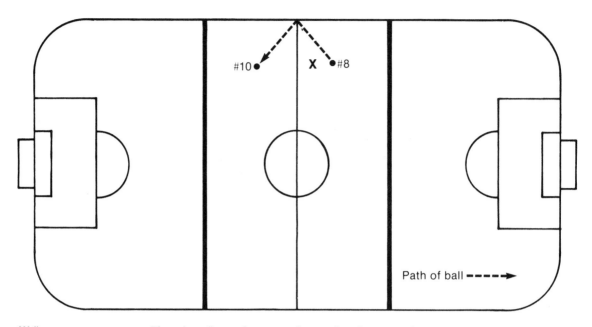

Wall passing to teammates. The side wall provides an excellent surface for give and go passing around a defender. Player #8, confronted by a defender X, simply directs the pass against the wall so that it rebounds to teammate #10 located in the space behind the defending player.

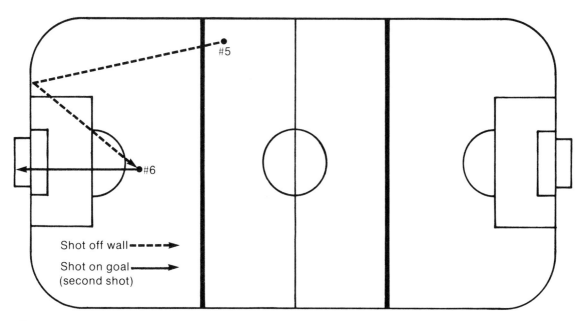

Shooting off the back wall. A player will purposely shoot wide of the goal so the ball rebounds to a teammate in a better scoring position. Player #5 shoots wide to draw out the goalkeeper as the ball rebounds to #6 in front of the goal. When playing indoors, the second shot is more likely to score.

Soccer

MISL playing field and players. Indoor soccer is played with five field players plus the goalkeeper. Using a 2-1-2 system, two defenders, one midfielder, and two forwards work collectively as a unit. When in possession of the ball, all players attack; when not in possession, all players defend. Indoor soccer requires the development of total players.

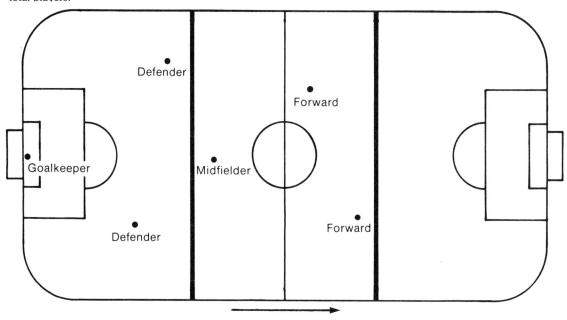

MISL Official Signals

Goal   Line pass   Kicking   Striking

Jumping   Handling ball   Holding   Pushing

Charging violently   Delay of   Indirect kick   Time out
Charging—behind   game penalty

Corner kick—point to corner
flag on side that kick
is to be taken

Obstruction—hit the   Unsportsmanlike conduct
chest with palms

Soccer

Players. Five field players plus a goalkeeper are usually on the field at one time. Unlimited substitution is permitted during the game. Players enter and leave the field while the game continues.

Officials. One referee has total control on the field. An alternate official supervises the timer's table, team benches, and penalty box. Goal judges are placed behind each goal to signal a score.

Game. It consists of 4 quarters, each 15 minutes in length. The clock does not stop except for the following:
- Ball goes out of play.
- Goal is scored.
- Red line violation.
- Penalty call.
- Penalty kick.
- Official's timeout.

After the ball leaves the playing area, play is resumed with a kick-in at the sideline where the ball left the playing area.

Scoring. The entire ball must cross the goal line for a goal to be scored.

MISL playing field demarcations and goal dimensions.

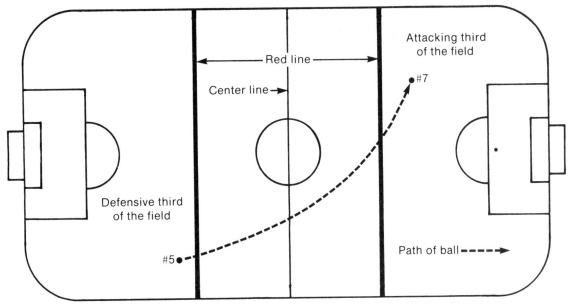

Red line violation. This violation is called when a player, #5, in the defensive third of the field makes a forward pass to a teammate, #7, in the attacking third of the field without being touched by another player in the middle third of the field. In this diagram, a violation has been committed. The opposing team is given possession of the ball with a free kick from the first crossed red line.

Penalties. A player is sent to the penalty box for the following offenses:

- Delay of game (2-minute penalty).
- Ungentlemanly conduct (2-minute penalty).
- Violent conduct (5-minute penalty plus ejection). When a player is serving time in the penalty box, his team must play a man short.

Major infractions are penalized by a direct free kick. If the infraction is severe, the player may also serve time in the penalty box. Minor infractions are penalized by an indirect free kick.

If, in the referee's judgment, a player is attempting to delay the game, the player will be required to serve 2 minutes in the penalty box. Delay of game is called for the following offenses:

- Player deliberately directing the ball over the perimeter wall.
- Too many players on the field.
- A field player, after receiving a throw from the goalkeeper, returns a kick back to his goalkeeper and the keeper handles the ball.
- On a free kick, defending players line up closer than 10 feet from the ball.

Soccer

When a defending player purposely commits a foul against an attacker in the penalty area, a penalty kick is awarded to the attacking team. The kick is taken from a spot 8 yards directly in front of the goal. Only the kicker and goalkeeper are allowed in the penalty area and arc when the kick is taken.

A red-line violation is indoor soccer's version of the offside rule. If a forward pass crosses both red lines in the air without being touched by another player, a red-line violation is called. An indirect kick from the first red line crossed restarts play.

A corner kick is awarded to the attacking team if the ball leaves the playing field between the two flags on the end line and is last touched by a player on the defending team.

10.The Future of American Soccer

Both indoor and outdoor versions of soccer, although differing slightly in certain rules and tactical play, are characterized by inherent qualities that attract players and spectators alike. Fluidity of motion coupled with total involvement of each individual provide a sport that generates excitement and enjoyment for those who participate. These basic attributes have made soccer the number one sport throughout the world, and these same qualities are sure to guarantee its continued popularity in the States. The future of the game looks very bright, as evidenced by its widespread acceptance at the youth, amateur, collegiate, and professional levels of play.

The burgeoning youth soccer movement is providing children with the opportunity to develop skills and gain valuable playing experience at an early age. Thousands of youngsters are playing in organized leagues throughout cities such as Tampa, Dallas, Portland, New York, and Tulsa. Many areas in which soccer had been previously nonexistent are now sponsoring organized youth associations under the guidance of the United States Soccer Federation. The young players will provide a solid base for the continued growth, development, and improvement in the standard of American soccer.

Women have discovered soccer's fascinations and are playing the game in ever-increasing numbers. It is reported to be the fastest-growing women's team sport in America, with an estimated 100,000 participants. At the present time, most teams are composed of adolescent girls, but women over the age of 19 years, primarily college students, are also playing in organized leagues throughout the country. The caliber of play is improving as more and more women actively participate as players rather than as passive spectators. In addition to the competition and excitement that soccer provides, the resultant health benefits are an added appeal for most women. With many interested mothers now coaching in youth leagues, women are becoming as familiar with soccer tactics and strategy as their male counterparts. Often a soccer game embraces whole families.

The Joseph P. Kennedy Jr. Foundation has organized and sponsored an extensive Special Olympics program for handicapped children interested in playing soccer. Instructional clinics and coaching workshops have been supported by the United States Soccer Federation as well as the North American Soccer League. Many professional players have volunteered their time and energy for instruction and personal appearances. In an effort to increase interest in the game, the Special Olympics have created a Soccer Skills Contest for its participants. Special Olympians in more than 10,000 local Special Olympics programs are instructed and tested in skills such as dribbling, passing, ball juggling, and shooting. Competitions for the skills contests are held at the local, regional, and national levels.

In addition to the large number of players now involved, another significant factor in the overall growth of the game is the quality and availability of coaches. To aid in the training of a sufficient number of coaches to meet the demands of increased player participation, the United States Soccer Federation has organized and promoted a national system of coaching schools. Aspiring coaches desiring to learn the most recent technical and tactical concepts of soccer coaching, plus information concerning areas of physiology, nutrition, fitness, and sport psychology, are required to get classroom and on-the-field instruction. Each coach, in order to be licensed, must satisfactorily pass a series of written and field examinations covering all aspects of the game. More importantly, the system provides a standard of instruction for youth players that is similar across the entire country. If the U.S. is to develop into an international soccer power, a unified system of coaching is an absolute necessity to provide correct and up-to-date information. The improvement in the caliber of our soccer coaches may be the single most important development in American soccer.

The continued success of our professional leagues is another barometer that signals the emergence of soccer as a major sports spectacle in the U.S.A. In addition to providing an exciting and entertaining form of sport for our young athletes, many of the professional teams are actively promoting and sponsoring youth development programs. It is the responsibility of our professional organizations to devote both time and money for the continued growth of these programs, not only for their own interests but also to provide impetus for further expansion and development in the years ahead.

In the upcoming decades, the dream of America's emergence as the guiding force of international soccer will surely be realized. There is no doubt that in the near future, the United States will develop world-class soccer of the same caliber that today exists in Germany or Brazil. Our athletes are perhaps the best in the world, and if we direct our efforts toward a goal, we will succeed in whatever we attempt. How soon we reach that desired level of play depends upon how quickly we can unify our efforts on a national basis. It is necessary to establish our own style and concept of soccer, choosing the best ingredients from various styles of play found throughout the world. The continued development of our amateur and professional leagues will play an important role, providing opportunity for increased participation at all levels.

Regardless of which level of play, the primary reason for playing soccer is the enjoyment derived from participation. As both former and present players will attest, many memorable and rewarding moments will be experienced within the confines of a soccer field, experiences that will be remembered and cherished for a lifetime.

Glossary

accelerate off the mark The ability to change speeds from a stationary position to full speed in the shortest possible time.

advantage rule Exercised by the referee when, in his opinion, penalizing a rule infraction would give an unfair advantage to the team committing the foul. The referee instead signals continuation of play and does not call the penalty.

agility drills Exercises designed to improve quickness and fluidity of movement in players.

ASL American Soccer League.

attacker *See* forwards.

backheel Deceptive method of passing in which player steps over the ball and heels it backward to a supporting teammate.

balance in defense Proper defensive positioning providing support and depth in the defense.

ball-watching A common mistake among inexperienced defenders. Occurs when the defender is so intent in following the flight of the ball he forgets to mark his opponent tightly.

banana shot A shot that curves in flight due to the spinning motion of the ball.

bicycle kick *See* overhead kick.

blind-side run Person without the ball running outside of his opponent's field of vision in order to receive a pass. A method of off-the-ball running.

block tackle Using the inside of the foot to block the ball as an opponent attempts to dribble.

catenaccio A defense-oriented system of play originated in Italy. Catenaccio led to low-scoring games lacking creativity and gradually gained disfavor with spectators and players alike.

center circle A circle, 10 yards in radius, located at the center of the field. The initial kickoff plus restarts of play after a goal has been scored all take place in center circle.

center forward Front-line attacking player occupying the central portion of the field, usually functioning as the primary goal-scoring forward.

central striker *See* center forward.

charging *See* shoulder charge.

chip pass Method of striking the foot under the ball to direct it over an opponent to a teammate.

circuit training Method of training that requires a player to complete a series of stations located within the circuit, each station consisting of drills designed to improve fitness and skill levels.

clearance header A defensive heading. The ball is cleared out of the danger area near the goal, headed as far and as wide as possible to the wing positions.

collecting the ball *See* receiving the ball.

concentration in defense Defensive tactic of grouping defenders in the most dangerous areas in front of the goal, thus limiting the space available to opposing players in those critical areas.

corner kick Method of putting the ball in play by the attacking team after it has crossed the opponent's end line when last touched by an opponent.

Soccer

counterattack Once the defending team has gained possession of the ball, it must quickly initiate its attack toward the opposing goal.

cover Proper defensive support. As one defender challenges the opponent in possession of the ball, he must be supported from behind by a teammate in the event the first defender is beaten.

cramp Involuntary contractions of a muscle. May be caused by a variety of reasons including, but not limited to, poor nutritional habits, fatigue, and injury to a muscle.

defenders *See* fullback.

defensive wall Defending players form a wall, usually composed of 3–4 players, to aid in defense against a free kick. The wall must be formed at least 10 yards from the ball.

deflection Sudden change in direction of the flight of the ball.

depth Proper support from behind by teammates, both in attack and defense.

diagonal Run designed to penetrate the defense while drawing opponents away from their central positions.

direct free kick Any free kick that can be scored directly without first touching another player.

distribution Methods by which the goalkeeper initiates the attack after he has gained control of the ball. The most common methods of distribution are throwing or kicking the ball to a teammate.

diving Technique used when a goalkeeper must leave his feet to save a shot at goal.

drop ball When play has been stopped by the referee for reasons other than a penalty, the play is restarted by dropping the ball between two opposing players. The ball cannot be played until it has first touched the ground.

drop kick Method of goalkeeper distribution in which he drops the ball and, just as it strikes the ground, kicks it downfield.

economical training A training scheme that incorporates fitness, skill, and tactical training within the same practice session.

end line Line marking the boundary at each end of the field.

endurance training Training regimen designed to prepare a player to function at maximum efficiency for the entire 90-minute (plus overtime) match.

far post run A run directed toward the far upright (goal post) on the opposite side of the field from the ball. Such a run away from the ball moves the attacker into a dangerous goal-scoring position as the ball is crossed to the far post.

fartlek Continuous endurance form of training consisting of long-distance running at various speeds.

FIFA Fédération International de Football Association; the ruling body of international soccer.

finesse Execution of soccer skills with smoothness and precision.

finish The end result of every successful attack; a score.

flexibility training Exercises for increasing a player's range of motion.

four-step rule Applies to goalkeepers who are in possession of the ball. The goalkeeper is not permitted to take more than four steps when holding, bouncing, or throwing the ball without releasing it so it may be played by another player. Violation of this rule is penalized by awarding an indirect free kick to the opposition at the location where the foul occurred.

forwards Players who occupy the front attacking positions, usually consisting of strikers and wingers.

fullbacks Players occupying the defensive positions in front of the goalkeeper. Most modern systems of play use four fullbacks, usually referred to as defenders.

full volley Striking the ball while it is still in the air. The instep is the most common surface of the foot used in volleying.

functional training Isolating the techniques and tactics of a certain playing position and stressing them in the practice session. An example of functional training for a central defender might be clearance headers to specified targets.

give-and-go pass Combination passing where one player passes to another and then moves to receive an immediate return pass. Sometimes called the wall pass.

goalkeeper The only player who is permitted use of the hands and arms when controlling and distributing the ball within the penalty area. His primary functions are to prevent goals by the opposition and to initiate the counterattack once he gains possession of the ball.

goal kick Method of restarting play after the ball goes over the defending team's end line last touched by the attacking team. The goal kick is taken from a point 6 yards in front of the defending team's goal.

goal side Proper defensive positioning. Defender must always position himself between his goal and the opponent he is marking.

grids Confined areas in which soccer skills and tactics may be practiced. Reducing the playing area through the use of grids increases the difficulty of execution.

halfbacks See midfielders.

half volley Striking the ball just at the moment it touches the ground.

heel pass See backheel.

high pressure Playing style that advocates pressuring the opponents in all sections of the field. Teams ap-

plying high pressure hope to cause mistakes by the opposing team.

indirect free kick A free kick from which a goal cannot be scored directly. Before entering the goal, the ball must be touched by a player other than the initial kicker.

inside of the foot Area on the inside surface of the foot between the ankle and toes, used in short- and medium-range passing.

instep The surface of the foot covered by the laces of the shoe. Usually used for long-range passing and power shooting.

interval training Endurance training regimen that alternates short intervals of high-intensity work with rest intervals, a rhythm closely simulating the actual physical demands of the match.

juggling Using all of the various body surfaces (i.e., feet, thigh, chest, shoulders, head, etc.), except the hands, to juggle the ball in the air without allowing it to touch the ground. Juggling is often used as a warm-up exercise.

kickboard Wall constructed for the practice of soccer skills. The individual player may pass or shoot the ball off the wall and then receive the rebound.

killing the ball Taking the pace off a passed ball as you receive it.

libero See sweeper.

lineman One of two people who aid the referee in officiating a soccer match. One lineman is assigned to patrol each side of the field (touchline).

linkmen See midfielders.

low pressure Style of play that allows the opposing players time and space in which to operate in their defending and midfield zones. However, as the opposing team moves forward into the attacking third of the field, their players are more tightly marked and available space is reduced.

Soccer

man-to-man coverage Defensive system in which each man is responsible for marking a particular opponent.

midfielders Players who occupy the positions in the central portions of the field. Also called halfbacks or linkmen. They connect the attack and the defense.

mobility Purposeful movement, both with and without the ball, serving to create space for teammates and to draw opponents into unfavorable positions.

MISL Major Indoor Soccer League.

NASL North American Soccer League.

near-post run Player, in an attempt to receive a pass, makes a run towards the goalpost nearest the location of the ball.

offside position If a player is in a technically offside position but is not interfering or involved with an opponent, the referee should not call the penalty since the player in question is not seeking to gain unfair advantage by being offside.

offside rule At the instant the ball is played, a player must have two opponents, including the goalkeeper, between himself and the opposing goal; otherwise, he is offside and is penalized by an indirect free kick awarded to the opposing team. A player cannot be offside if the ball was last played by an opponent, the player is in his own half of the field, or he received the ball from a corner kick, throw-in, goal kick, or drop-ball situation.

offside trap Defensive tactic in which defenders, after playing the ball upfield, quickly move forward to leave opponents in an offside position. If these opponents then receive the ball, they will be termed offside and penalized.

one-touch passing Interpasssing among players without stopping the ball; also called first-time passing.

overhead kick Player swings both legs upward to strike the ball as it travels above his head. Also called the bicycle kick, this is a very acrobatic method of scoring goals.

overlap When a team is in possession of the ball, a supporting teammate will run from behind into a forward position to receive the pass. The overlap is an excellent method of moving defenders into attacking positions for a strike at goal. Overlapping defenders typify modern soccer tactics that stress both attacking and defending capabilities in all players.

own goal Occurs when a member of the defending team inadvertently directs the ball into his own goal, scoring against his team.

passing Directing the ball to a teammate. Many body surfaces may be used in passing, including the inside of the foot, instep, outside of the foot, heel, toe, and head.

penalty arc An arc drawn with a 10-yard radius from the penalty spot. No one, except the kicker, is allowed within the area of the arc and the penalty area when the penalty kick is being taken.

penalty area Area located in front and to the sides of the goal in which the goalkeeper is allowed use of the hands in controlling the ball. The area measures 44 yards wide by 18 yards deep.

penalty kick Direct free kick awarded to the attacking team if a defender commits a major foul within his own penalty area. The kick is taken from the penalty spot, located 12 yards directly in front of the goal.

pendulum training Soccer ball suspended from a rope, useful for skill practice. The height of the ball may be varied for passing with the feet, heading, etc.

penetrating pass See through pass.

pitch See playing field.

playing field Rectangular playing surface 100-130 yards long and 50-100 yards wide.

poke tackle Reaching in and, using the toe, kicking the ball away from an opponent.

possession Stringing together a number of passes among members of the same team; not allowing the opposition to gain control of the ball.

punching The goalkeeping technique of punching balls out of the goal area. Punching is used on high air balls that the goalkeeper cannot safely catch. Rather than risk dropping the ball in the goal area, the keeper uses one or both fists to direct the ball out of the danger area.

quick turn The ability of a player to receive a pass with his back to the opponent's goal, turn, and play it forward, all executed in one fluid motion.

receiving the ball The art of collecting a pass and bringing it under control. The ball may be received on various body surfaces including the inside of the foot, instep, sole of the foot, outside of the foot, thigh, chest, and head.

red card Presented when, in the referee's judgment, a player must be ejected from the game for violation of the rules governing play.

referee The person who is responsible for officiating the soccer game. Two linemen assist the referee.

restarts Methods of beginning play after a stoppage in action. Restarts include direct and indirect free kicks, throw-ins, corner kicks, goal kicks, and the drop ball.

rhythm The tempo or pace of a soccer game.

running off the ball Purposeful running when not in possession of the ball to create space for teammates. Intelligent running off the ball is a requirement in modern soccer.

save Goalkeeper prevents an opponent's shot from entering the goal for a score.

scissors kick *See* overhead kick.

screening When in possession of the ball, a player must keep his body in a position between the opponent and the ball, in effect screening his opponent. Also called shielding, this skill is very important in maintaining ball possession.

shielding *See* screening.

shin guards Light, protective pads worn over the front portion of the lower leg to help prevent injuries.

shooting Directing the ball at the opponent's goal in an effort to score, either by kicking or heading.

shoulder charge Legal tactic used when challenging an opponent for the ball.

side volley Striking the ball, bouncing or traveling in the air, while it is located to the side of the player.

slide tackle Method of dislodging the ball from an opponent by sliding into the ball and kicking it away.

square pass A pass made across the field. Often used to slow the tempo of the game or to set up a penetrating pass.

stamina Endurance; the ability to perform at a high work rate for an extended period.

static stretching Method of increasing player flexibility. Muscles are stretched to their greatest extent and held in that position for 15-30 seconds. Bouncing in an attempt to increase stretching is not advisable since injury may result.

stopper One of the central defenders in the standard four-man back line. The stopper usually plays in front of the sweeper and marks the opposing center forward.

Soccer

striker Front running, attacking player who is usually one of the primary goal scorers of the team. Also called forward.

substitution Replacing a field player or the goal-keeper with another player.

support Tactical term implying movement of players towards the ball to aid the teammate in possession. Proper support will provide passing options to the player in possession, likewise reducing his chances of losing the ball.

sweeper The last defender, given the responsibility to support the fullback line. He sweeps behind the defense, cutting off penetrating passes to goal. Also called libero.

systems Organization of players on the field. Defenders are listed first, then midfielders, and finally the forwards. For example, the 4-3-3 system consists of 4 defenders, 3 midfielders, and 3 attackers. The goal-keeper is not included in the numbering.

tackling Using the feet to steal the ball from an opponent. *See* block tackle, slide tackle, poke tackle.

tactics Organizational concept of how individuals, groups, or an entire team of players function together.

target man Striker who is used as the principal target for passes originating from defenders and midfield players. The ball is played forward to the target who then distributes it to an open teammate or goes at goal himself.

technique Skill training; includes heading, shooting, dribbling, and receiving balls.

throw-in Method of restarting play after the ball has traveled outside of the touchlines. Player must throw it into play using two hands directly over his head. Both feet must be kept on the ground when releasing the ball.

total soccer Concept of play stressing all around players who can both defend and attack. When in possession, all players attack; after loss of possession, all players defend. When playing total soccer, rigid positioning is nonexistent.

touchline Side boundary lines of the field. If the ball goes completely over the touchline, it is put into play by a throw-in.

two-touch passing Method of interpassing in which a player receiving the ball uses his first touch to control it and the second touch to pass the ball to a teammate.

volley *See* full volley, half volley, side volley.

wall pass Combination passes between two teammates. One player serves as a wall to redirect the path of the ball. The player with the ball passes off the wall and then sprints into open space to receive the return pass.

warm-up Exercises that physiologically prepare the body for a strenuous training session or actual match play.

width in attack Attacking tactic of using the entire width of the field in an attempt to draw defending players away from the central positions of the field.

wingbacks Fullbacks who play on the flanks of the defense, usually marking the opposing wingers.

wingers Forwards who operate on the flank positions near the touchlines.

work rate Level of physical exertion a player demonstrates throughout the game.

World Cup International tournament of soccer, the final games of which are held every 4 years.

yellow card Issued by the referee to a player who is guilty of violation of the laws concerning conduct of play during a game. A second warning (red card) constitutes ejection from the match.

zonal defense Defensive system in which each player is responsible for marking the opposing player(s) in a certain section of the playing field.

Index

Soccer